Lapwing

The Farm

Paddock

Poplar Meadow

...eadow

Poplar Glades

...ckthorn Thickets
& Glades

East Meadow

Bridleway

Brock's Pit

A SECRET LANDSCAPE

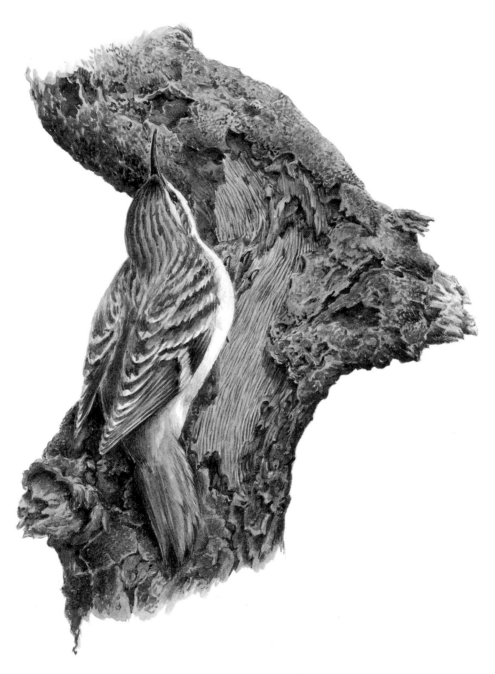

A Treecreeper searches for
insects among crevices in the
bark of a dead tree.

Flowers of high summer.

A SECRET LANDSCAPE

Diary of Lapwing Meadows

BY BENJAMIN PERKINS

Century
London   Melbourne   Auckland   Johannesburg

Also by Benjamin Perkins: Trees, published in 1984

First published in 1986
by Century Hutchinson Limited
Brookmount House
62-65 Chandos Place,
London WC2N 4NW

British Library Cataloguing in Publication Data

Perkins, Benjamin
    A secret landscape: a diary of Lapwing Meadows.
    1. Meadow flora __ England __ Suffolk
    2. Meadow flora __ England __ Suffolk
    I. Title
    574.9426'4   QH138.S7/

ISBN 0-7126-1221-1

Produced and designed by
Savitri Books Ltd
71, Great Russell Street
London WC1B 3BN

Managing editor and art direction:
Mrinalini Srivastava
Editor: John Gilbert

Set in Palatino by Dorchester Typesetting, Dorchester
Reproduction by Gateway Platemakers, London
Printed and bound in Hong Kong by Mandarin Offset

Title page. Creeping Jenny.

Opposite. The fungus
Pleurotus cornucopiae.

A word is called for on the use of capital initials with the names of animals and plants in
this book. Modern usage, though tending to favour their disuse, is not entirely
consistent. With the exception of domestic animals and a few very similar species such
as the rabbit and the fox, I have used a capital with the names of species, though not for
groups. Thus *Welted Thistle, Redwing* and *Painted Lady* have a capital, while *nettles,
thrushes* and *plume moth* do not. My own preference for the use of capitals has a practical
reason: I spend a lot of time consulting natural history books and I have often deplored
the difficulty of finding a word among a page of text. The use of a capital initial causes it
to spring instantly into view, and saves a great deal of time and frustration.

For Bobby and Di

CONTENTS

Robin's Pin-cushion Gall or
Bedeguar and Pea Galls on
Dog Rose.

INTRODUCTION

I n north Essex, not many miles from the River Stour which forms the boundary between Essex and Suffolk, and approached by a series of narrow and winding lanes, there lies a string of five small meadows with an adjoining wood and spinney. The meadows all have individual names but the whole area is known locally as Lapwing Meadows and it provides a pleasant contrast to the surrounding arable fields. Thirty years ago such an area of land would have been quite unremarkable; today, because of agricultural policies which have resulted in the wholesale destruction of woods and hedgerows, the drainage of wetlands and the ploughing-up of grassland, it is something of a rarity.

Rabbit stretching.

It is a sobering statistic that since 1940 no less than ninety-five per cent of lowland herb-rich meadows in this country have been lost to the plough or the bulldozer, and of the remaining five per cent just under half have been to some extent damaged. Most of the tiny handful of unspoilt meadows left to us have only been saved through purchase or lease, in the nick of time, by bodies such as the county trusts for nature conservation.

For years I have observed the disappearance of old meadowland and of the important habitat it provides and I felt that there was little time to lose if I were to carry out the project I had in mind. I wanted to record all that I could observe of the fauna and flora present on an area of meadowland in my part of the world, keeping a field diary and painting some of the typical, uncommon or particularly attractive species of plants and flowers. I decided to start my observations in April 1984, ending in March of the following year. Lapwing Meadows were ideal from my point of view, for they are occupied by friends who farm in a neighbouring parish and the area is sufficiently close to my house to be easily accessible in all weathers. For several years I had been in the habit of taking walks there at intervals, always deriving great enjoyment from the rather unkempt state of the fields which encourages a profusion of plant and animal species. I hope something of the great sense of peace and contentment I always feel on the meadows comes over in this book.

Lapwing Meadows have not escaped unscathed from the hands of the improver: both East Meadow and Rush Meadow grew arable crops towards the end of the war, and the whole area was ploughed through and reseeded to grass in 1949. Since then, however, they have received no intensive fertiliser or herbicide treatment; more importantly, the parts of the two central meadows lying on the south side of the brook have never been ploughed and the marshy area on Peticote Meadow remains in its natural, undrained state. The reseeded areas have been colonised afresh by a variety of wild flowers, many of which doubtless lingered in the hedge bottoms and spread back into the meadows when the opportunity arose.

Besides the meadows themselves, there are other congenial habitats for both plants and animals, including the two adjacent woods, the Blackthorn thickets on Peticote, the stream that runs the length of the meadows and more than two miles of ancient and well-treed hedgerows.

In the past these hedgerows were no doubt cut back and kept trimmed and stockproof. I have been unable to detect any signs of former layering – and indeed the art of hedge-laying was never much practised in this area – but some of the large trees, particularly the oaks and Ashes, show signs of having formerly been pollarded while huge and knobbly Hazel stools bear witness to regular coppicing over a long period. Pollarding is the practice, formerly very common, of cutting trees back to between six and twelve feet from ground level. The poles thus obtained were used for a great variety of farm and craft purposes, and the trees would shoot again. Regular pollarding had the effect of prolonging the life of trees, in the case of oaks almost indefinitely; and most of the oldest oaks now living have been pollarded in the past. Coppicing has a similar purpose, but is used to obtain smaller poles, and the trees or bushes are cut back to ground level.

For several decades the hedges have been allowed to grow at will, becoming massive and rampant, though often hollow in their bottoms, necessitating the additional use of barbed wire fencing to prevent stock from breaking out.

Ponies grazing on Peticote Meadow.

From 1949 until the 1960s the meadows were grazed by horses and dairy cows; after that, when the milking herds had been dispersed, by bullocks and horses. In recent years, with scant profits from fattening bullocks on grass, the meadows have been grazed solely by horses (presently by three or four hunters and about nine ponies). One meadow is shut up each spring for hay, and at the same time the more accessible parts of all the meadows are chain-harrowed and given a light top-dressing of nitrogenous fertiliser. Herbicide sprays are occasionally used to subdue the more obdurate patches of thistle and nettle, though not during the year under review.

The area is shot over several times during the winter months, some two hundred pheasant poults being reared in release pens in Brock's Pit and the Spinney each year, to augment the native stock. Whatever one's views regarding the ethics of field sports, many of the remaining small woods, roughs, hedges, ponds and plantations are still in existence and provide habitats for numerous creatures besides the quarry species only on account of the shooting interest.

The meadows form a chain, just over a mile long, on an east-west axis, and cover an area of nearly thirty acres. Their northern boundary is marked for the length of East Meadow by a small lane which continues alongside the other four meadows in the form of an old green road; bridleways branch off the road to the south between East Meadow and Poplar and between Peticote and Spinney Meadow. The stream runs from west to east along the southern side of Rush and Spinney Meadows and through the others. It starts as little more than a ditch, but its volume is increased, all along its route, by tributary ditches and land drains, so that by the time it reaches East Meadow it warrants the title, which I have generally given it, of 'the brook'.

To the south of East Meadow is Brock's Pit Wood, and adjoining the marsh on Peticote is the Spinney; these two small woods complete the area of our survey, and I will now describe the individual parts in greater detail.

EAST MEADOW

East Meadow, about seven acres in extent, is divided diagonally by the brook into two roughly triangular sections. Botanically, it is the least interesting of the meadows, being well drained and made up chiefly of respectable grasses such as Perennial Ryegrass (the dominant species), Meadow Fescue, Cocksfoot, Timothy, Meadow Foxtail and Smooth Meadow Grass, with much less of the Sweet Vernal Grass and various wetland species that abound on the other meadows. In recent years it has

*Opposite. A pair of Redpolls and a cock Siskin on
Alder. The two species feed together in small flocks
and are seen on the meadows from February to April.*

been cut for hay (generally quite late in the summer), the horses being turned back on to it after the hay has been gathered, to graze the aftermath. There are trees (including some large Ashes, willows and Alders and a few Sycamores) all along the brook, and the roadside hedge is particularly luxuriant with huge Hawthorn bushes, great mounds of Bramble and many tall oaks and Field Maples. The Bramble mounds consist of dense, compacted layers of dead material with new, leafy growth arching over the top – ideal cover for rabbits; and in spring, Primroses and Violets grow in profusion all along the foot of the hedge.

POPLAR MEADOW

A narrow bridleway divides East Meadow and Poplar and continues along the edge of Brock's Pit. In the angle that it forms with the brook there stands the splendid old native Black Poplar – a rare species today – which gives its name to the meadow. Its massive trunk and all its main limbs are encrusted with woody burrs, and its crown rears up over a hundred feet, dwarfing all the trees around it. Also notable are the two great oak trees that stand just to the right of the gate, their spreading branches casting a shade much appreciated by the horses in hot weather.

The meadow is divided down its length by the brook, with about two and a half acres on the north side and one and a half acres on the south. At some time in the past an attempt was made to straighten the brook, but for what purpose it is difficult to see, since the cut-off meanders were never filled in and now form a series of shallow ponds on the south side of the brook.

Unlike cattle and sheep, which graze and spread their droppings indiscriminately over a pasture, horses graze certain areas and dung in others; all the meadows therefore have stretches of close-cropped turf alternating with areas made up of coarse grasses, Stinging Nettles, thistles, docks, etc. On Poplar the dunging areas tend to be alongside the hedges and the brook, with the grazing areas in the middle, and in summer the short turf is initially bright with Daisies and Buttercups and later with the purple flowers of Self-heal. The area on the south side of the brook is narrower and bushier, and as summer proceeds, the coarser herbage encroaches on the grazing areas until separate grassy glades

The old Black Poplar tree on
Poplar Meadow.

appear, connected only by narrow tracks through the man-high vegetation. The central glade is very wet, the sward full of Flote Grass mixed with various rushes and sedges.

PETICOTE MEADOW

P eticote is the largest of the meadows, and botanically the most interesting, since it includes the marsh. Like Poplar, it is divided down its length by the brook, but the area on the north side is much larger, sloping from the green road down to the brook, and covering seven acres. The remaining three acres, on the south side of the brook, consist largely of dense Blackthorn thickets enclosing a series of flowery glades; and rising out of the thickets, along the brookside, are Alders, White and Crack Willows, Sallows, Crab Apples and a few Black Italian Poplars. Following the southern edge of the thickets is a steep bank in which are badger setts, used also at times by foxes, and numerous rabbit burrows.

The marsh lies at the west end of the meadow, on either side of the brook, and covers an area of about an acre and a half. The part on the north side of the brook I have called the Orchid bog, from the profusion of Common Spotted Orchids that grow there in early summer. It consists chiefly of a bed of Lesser Pond Sedge, the ground rising slightly towards the middle where there is a large domed Sallow bush and a Crack Willow that is slowly dying – willows like to be able to reach out for water, but will not tolerate permanently waterlogged roots. The section of brook running through the marsh was, in the past, straightened and banked up on either side, presumably in order to prevent flooding. Fortunately it did not have the effect of drying out the marsh, which remains waterlogged even in the driest summer weather.

Opposite. Typical marsh flowers in July include
Marsh Bird's-foot Trefoil and Water Mint while the
Yellow Meadow Vetchling (on the right) is found
around the edges of the marsh and in the thicket
glades. The Small Skipper butterfly and Azure
Damselfly are seen chiefly in the marsh area.

The Iris bog, on the other side of the brook, is more extensive and dominated by a bed of Yellow Flag Iris which makes a splendid show in June. Mixed among the Iris and flowering at the same time are Ragged Robin and Lesser Pond Sedge, while later in the year Willow-herb, Marsh Bird's-foot Trefoil, Hemp Agrimony and Wild Angelica are prominent. Where the marsh is shaded by the Spinney, the Iris peters out and is replaced by Reed Canary Grass. Around the whole area, and indeed in the wetter parts of all the meadows, is Water Mint which scents the air deliciously throughout the summer months.

SPINNEY MEADOW

This is a small, rectangular meadow of just under two acres, bounded on one side by the green road and on the other by the Spinney. A bridleway runs between it and Peticote.

It is very sheltered, being surrounded on all sides by tall trees, and is a good meadow both for flowers and, in the autumn, fungi. In the green road hedge are half-a-dozen fine young oaks; I hope they still preside over as tranquil a scene when they reach their prime, a hundred years hence.

RUSH MEADOW

This meadow is long and thin, narrowing to a sharp point at its western end, and covers about five acres. The brook runs along its southern boundary in a deep, wide channel with a gravelly bottom, overhung and sometimes hidden by sprawling bushes of Hazel, thorn, Dog Rose and the like. It is a wet meadow, particularly at its eastern end where there is an old horsepond and several flashes – depressions in the ground which become shallow pools after rain. The squelchy ground around these flashes is a favourite feeding place for Snipe which winter on the meadows in considerable numbers, a pair occasionally staying to breed. Two-thirds of the way down the green road hedge, an oak and a Field Maple have grown up side by side and have become fused at the base of the trunk so that the tree appears to be half oak and half maple.

In dry summers the stream above the Spinney (where it is joined by tributaries) sometimes dries out completely, but the pond always holds water. It teems with life, including large numbers of Smooth Newts which gather there to breed in the spring.

Remote from any road and surrounded by large arable fields, Spinney and Rush Meadows are among the quietest and most peaceful spots to be found anywhere in the district.

THE GREEN ROAD

This is a very ancient trackway, probably dating from long before the Norman Conquest. It is sunken between banks from which grow a wide variety of trees and shrubs, possibly remnants of the original wildwood that must once have covered the entire area. Pedunculate Oak and Field Maple are the predominant tree species, though as many elms were once present; all mature elms are now dead as a result of Dutch Elm disease, but there are still some young Smooth-leaved Elms (up to thirty-five feet) and a considerable amount of sucker growth, as well as a few young Wych Elms. Ash, Crab Apple, Hazel, Blackthorn, Hawthorn and Elder are all there in abundance, and Sallow, Spindle Tree and Purging Buckthorn occur at fairly regular intervals. Dog Rose and Bramble are both plentiful, Field Rose and Downy Rose less so, though there are several good examples of both species on Rush Meadow. There is one bush of Guelder Rose (and another in the thickets). Among the climbers, Ivy and Traveller's Joy are abundant and there is a quantity of Wild Hop towards the far end of Rush. In the continuation of the green road, beyond the meadows, there is plenty of Dogwood, but on the meadows themselves I found only one bush, and that down in the thickets.

Riders use the green road in sufficient numbers, particularly in summer, to prevent it becoming overgrown. Otherwise it is little frequented, and often, as I have walked back to my car in the dusk of a summer evening, with Tawny Owls hooting from the Spinney and bats flitting over the meadows, I have reflected on how different it must once have been, plied by teams of horses and, earlier still, of oxen, and echoing to the voices of hunters, peddlers, gipsies, drovers with their flocks and herds, men-at-arms perhaps, and villagers trudging through the mire to visit kinsfolk in distant hamlets.

Badger in Brock's Pit.

BROCK'S PIT

Brock's Pit is a wood of some eight and three-quarter acres planted on a north-facing slope around a large, long-disused sandpit. Some parts were formerly made up mainly of Smooth-leaved Elms, nearly all of which are now dead, many of them fallen and rotting on the forest floor. Otherwise, the predominant tree species is Sycamore, mixed with a fair quantity of Common Oak, Ash and Field Maple. There are a few tall old

Norway Spruces, the odd European Larch and a number of Horse Chestnuts around the south edge of the wood. On its eastern border are several large Crab Apples and a stand of still apparently healthy Wych Elms. The understorey is made up of Hazel, Hawthorn, Blackthorn, Elder, etc., and the floor of the wood is carpeted, in spring, with such plants as Dog's Mercury, Red Campion, Ground Ivy, Fox-tail Feather Moss and Tamarisk-leaved Feather Moss, and in summer with an inpenetrable forest of Stinging Nettles. Bracken occurs in a few places in open glades and around the borders of the wood.

At the bottom of the wood is a splendid Hazel, forty-three feet high, with multiple stems spreading out around it to a diameter of more than fifty feet; and near the head of the pit is an unusually large Buckthorn tree branching out into a wide crown from a short single bole two and a half feet in diameter. Other large Buckthorns are growing near by.

The working face and sides of the old pit are tall and steep, and trees growing from the bottom of it rise up a hundred feet on slim, unbranched stems, barely surmounting its rim.

In the centre of the wood is the pheasant release pen and near by is a group of badger setts that are in regular use.

Wood Pigeon.

THE SPINNEY

The Spinney is a small, very wet wood, about two acres in extent, made up principally of Alder, Ash and Crack Willow, with a few very fine old Black Italian Poplars and some oak and Field Maple at its drier southern edge. Two drainage ditches run through it to join the brook, and the understorey includes Hazel, Elder, Sallow and Red Currant.

To the west of the Spinney is a small area of rough grass and rushes recently planted with Alders and Poplars.

THE SURROUNDING FIELDS

T he land surrounding the meadows is arable apart from a narrow paddock running down to the meadows from the farmstead. In accordance with current practice, most of it is sown to winter wheat or winter barley, and in the year under review only the field below the Lodge was sown with spring barley. After harvest, the next field to the east was left under stubble until the end of the shooting season when winter beans were broadcast and ploughed in. The fields to the south of the meadows are large, most of the hedges having been removed long ago and the ditches filled in, but on the north side the fields are divided by good hedges and ditches, with trees at sensible intervals, to the great benefit not only of the game, but of all forms of wildlife. The soil, in the valley, consists of alluvial deposits, sands and gravels, while that of the surrounding fields is predominantly chalky boulder clay.

D uring the year of this survey, I visited the meadows at least once a week, generally twice a week through the summer months, and encountered hardly any species of plant or animal which could be described as a rarity, though a few merited the description 'uncommon'. What the meadows did provide was an abundance and variety of species, within a comparatively small area of land. Most of these would still be quite common, given suitable habitats, but many are nowadays unfamiliar even to country people because their habitat has been destroyed; Ragged Robin and the Common Spotted Orchid, both species confined to marshy situations, are good examples.

Some species have vanished entirely, or become very rare during the past two decades, as a result of farming practice. There must have been a time when Corncrakes were heard from the meadows and the surrounding cornfields, but these have long since vanished and only occur in the county now as occasional passage migrants. The Grey Partridge has been declining steadily in numbers and is now very scarce, while the Barn

Opposite. The vivid, yellow flowers of Kingcup or
Marsh Marigold form large clumps in the marsh and
along the banks of the brook in May.

Owl has disappeared from the immediate neighbourhood during the five years that I have lived in my present house. Frogs and Toads began their swift decline back in the 1960s and are now confined almost entirely to garden ponds in built-up areas, where they are not affected by agricultural chemical run-off. As I walked the meadows in early spring, it still seemed unnatural, almost unbelievable, that not a single pond or ditch held spawn or tadpoles.

Other species remain quite widely distributed, but at a much lower density than before, the Hare being one good example and the Grass Snake another. When I first came to live in Essex, twenty-five years ago, there were places near my house where I could be fairly confident of seeing Grass Snakes on almost any sunny, summer day. This particular summer I was delighted to see two in my garden (I had seen only one there during the previous four years) but in all my wanderings around the meadows I saw just one specimen. In comparison with these meagre sightings, it is interesting to read John Clare, the Northamptonshire poet (1793–1864), who wrote that 'it was a very common thing among the people of the villages round to go in the fens a-snake catching and carry home large sticks of them strung like eels on osiers which the French men [prisoners from the Napoleonic wars] woud readily buy as an article of very palatable food'. I wonder if there is anywhere in England, nowadays, where one could find snakes in such numbers?

I get the impression, too, that Cuckoos are now far fewer; it was 3rd June before I first heard one calling from the meadows, and despite a teeming population of small birds, I heard only the occasional Cuckoo through the rest of the summer. I am not indulging in nostalgic hyperbole when I say that in my youth scarcely a May or June day would pass without the sound of a Cuckoo call.

To set against these losses, there have been a few gains; one success story (for which I have no explanation) is that of the Hornet. This very large and handsome wasp was a rare species when I first came to live in the county in 1959. In twenty years I saw but one specimen, and once found an empty nest in a fallen elm. Yet in 1979 there was a population explosion and in every year since then they have been abundant. I came across Hornets frequently during my walks on the meadows, particularly towards the end of summer.

The most pleasant surprise during my year's ramblings was the

Long-tailed Tits.

quantity of butterflies frequenting the meadows. I recorded twenty different species, and there were many days during that (exceptionally warm) summer when they were present in vast numbers. On one August day, standing still, I counted thirty-four Gatekeepers on thistle heads within a few yards of me; and on other days there were just as many Small Tortoiseshells or Meadow Browns. The migrant butterflies were late arriving and less abundant than usual, but I think that, with the exception of the Speckled Wood, the Ringlet, the White-letter Hairstreak and the Essex Skipper, I saw every Essex butterfly that I could reasonably expect to see, that is, excluding rare, vagrant or localised species.

I have recorded all the mammals, birds, butterflies, dragonflies and damselflies, and flowering plants that I encountered. With other groups I have been more selective, mentioning only those species that were particularly prominent, or that seemed of special interest. I had neither the time nor the expertise to attempt the identification of all the insects, spiders, mosses, fungi, etc. that I saw; and, in any event, this would merely have resulted in a long list of Latin names. In fact, I have avoided the use of scientific names as far as possible in the text, using them only where no common name exists; but for the sake of accuracy, both the common and scientific names of all species mentioned are listed in the Systematic List of Species at the back of the book.

APRIL

Kingfisher by the brook.

My first walk round all the meadows was made at the beginning of April, when winter still held sway and signs of spring were few and far between. It was not a very cold day, but it was grey, raw and cheerless, with the wind in the east, and the rain falling steadily out of an unsmiling sky. The meadow grass was cropped short by the horses that had been wintered on it, and poached by their hooves, while the green road and the bridleways were deep in mud, the wheel-ruts brimming with dirty water. The trees stood bare and gaunt, rain dripping from branch to branch, their buds still tight-furled against the winter cold.

Even so, there were some portents of spring. In the sheltered hedge bottoms and on the banks of a deep ditch in East Meadow, there were Primroses in flower, and clumps of new, glossy-green and speckled leaves of Cuckoo Pint. Dog's Mercury was flowering in the woods and along the tree-shaded banks of the stream, while the ground beneath the Alder and Hazel trees was littered with their fallen orange-brown catkins.

I walked round both halves of East Meadow – which had already been chain-harrowed to spread the horse droppings and aerate the compacted soil – and then set off westwards, along the chain of meadows, a flock of Fieldfares flying ahead of me. Each time I caught up with them they would fly on another stage, calling to one another as they flew: 'cha-cha-chack, cha-cha-cha-chack.'

The horses on Poplar and on the two westerly meadows watched me rather dejectedly as I passed, the rain glistening on their long winter coats. Reaching the marsh, I put up a pair of Mallard which circled twice before flying away, and two or three Snipe, while a dozen or so very noisy Lapwing swooped over Peticote Meadow.

On my next visit, a few days later, it was pleasantly sunny, with a fresh, light breeze, following on a frosty morning. Buds on the Hazel and thorn trees were starting to swell. Lesser Celandine was in bloom and the first Kingcups were opening their splendid chrome-yellow flowers beside the stream. Fresh mole-hills dotted the low-lying ground and both adult and well-grown young rabbits sped into cover at my approach, all the way up the meadows. From Peticote I put up a pair of Red-legged Partridge, and from the marsh first a pair and then a wisp of twelve Snipe. I also surprised a couple of what I took to be Mallard, but as the drake flew past I glimpsed a big white patch on his breast and wondered

Alder trees and Primroses beside the brook on East Meadow in early April.

briefly if he was a Shoveler, although I had not noticed the characteristically huge beak. During the next few weeks I often saw this pair of ducks, and towards the end of the month, from the cover of the bridleway hedge, I got a good view of the drake through binoculars as he stood preening beside the stream. The female, presumably sitting by then, was a normal Mallard, but the drake was a very odd bird: shaped like a

Red Dead-nettle and a white form of the Sweet Violet,
seen here with the empty shell of a Garden Snail, add
further touches of colour to the April hedgerows.

Mallard, he had the typical bottle-green head and neck, curly tail feathers and grey and brown upper parts, but the neck-ring was replaced by that large, uneven, white breast patch, the speculum was green instead of purple, and the flanks and belly were a rich, dark chestnut. I wondered if he could be a Mallard Shoveler hybrid.

Other birds I noted that day included a Siskin on the mud beside the brook on Poplar Meadow and two pairs of Redpolls feeding on the grass near by, a Treecreeper on a dead Crack Willow on the marsh, a Goldcrest busy feeding in a Pussy Willow, and parties of Long-tailed Tits working their way down the hedges. A Yellowhammer by the gate into Poplar already had a bright yellow head, and in the nearby hedge I found a Blackbird's nest with two eggs. The sound of cock Pheasants calling and beating their wings could be heard from all sides. They looked splendid with their bright scarlet wattles and prominent ear tufts. Apart from the more common types – the ringnecked 'Mongolians' and ringless 'Old English' – I noticed a number of handsome melanistic mutants, with purplish or greenish-black plumage. Magpies and Jays were much in evidence – too much so judging from the number of empty thrush and Blackbird eggshells that I found – and there was a good volume of bird-song, mainly from Great and Blue Tits, Dunnocks, Blackbirds, Song Thrushes, Chaffinches and Skylarks. Oddly lacking throughout the first half of the month were the songs of either Chiffchaff or Willow Warbler. In most years I hear one or both during the first few days of April, often before the end of March, but this year it was mid-April before I heard and saw the first Willow Warbler; and although I heard a Chiffchaff near my house on 9th April, it was not until the 19th that I heard one from the meadows, singing somewhere in the depths of Brock's Pit. On the same day I saw my first Swallow (over Peticote) although I had been seeing them hawking for insects over the river for the past fortnight.

The 14th April was lovely, warm and sunny with a light south-westerly breeze, and it was the first day when insects appeared in any number. Bumble-bees and Honey Bees droned among the flowers of Ground Ivy and Red Dead-nettle, Peacock butterflies sunned themselves on the grass or fed, together with Commas, on Pussy Willow catkins, and a few Brimstones patrolled the bridleway hedge where Purging Buckthorn, their larval food plant, grew in abundance.

Sweet Violets, both white and purple, Lesser Celandine and Primroses were flowering beside the huge, overgrown hedges of East Meadow; I noticed some green buds, their centres pecked out, strewn under the Sycamores near Brock's Pit, and I presumed that Bullfinches were responsible. In Brock's Pit I found three species of violet in bloom: Sweet Violet, Early Dog Violet and, in the release pen, a single large clump of the very attractive Hairy Violet, with its large bluish-purple flowers.

On Poplar, I watched the Three-spined Sticklebacks, most of them still shoaled up in the deeper parts of the brook, the females already big with spawn and the males displaying their ruby gills and bellies. A freshly dead cock fish lay on the bed of the stream and I hooked it up with a stick and took it home to draw; it was a fine specimen, measuring two and three quarter inches, with nothing to indicate how it had met its end. Beside one of the meander ponds near by I found a partly eaten Smooth Newt, suggesting that others had already arrived there to breed.

Male Three-spined
Stickleback.

Entering Peticote via the Blackthorn thickets, I crept through dark and narrow tunnels between the bushes to inspect the badger setts in the bank for any signs of recent occupation, but found only the tracks and droppings of rabbits and foxes. Coming out of the thickets into the marsh, I was standing by the brook where it flows into Peticote from the Spinney, wondering what had just plopped loudly into the water, when I caught a movement out of the corner of my eye and turned in time to see a large Stoat bounding across the meadow from the thickets towards the bridleway, its head held very high, a baby rabbit in its mouth.

Opposite. Ground Ivy and Sweet Vernal Grass with a Green-veined White butterfly and, on a leaf of Ground Ivy, the Shieldbug Eysarcoris fabricii.

The first Cowslips were almost in flower on Peticote and overhead Lapwing swooped and tumbled in display flight, giving out their curious spring calls that start with a growl and end with a creaky version of their normal 'pee wee'. I heard the sound repeatedly over the next few weeks, as two pairs stayed to nest in the marsh, and one other pair, at least, near the far end of Rush.

From Peticote I entered the Spinney where I found the slots of Roe Deer very clear in the muddy banks of the ditches and caught a glimpse of a brownish bird, head pointed forwards, running through the undergrowth – almost certainly a Water Rail, though I could not focus my glasses in time to confirm this. Many of the Ash trees here were infested with Cramp Balls, a hard, black fungus whose appearance justifies its country name of King Alfred's Cakes.

Three species of violet are found in Brock's Pit. From left to right Hairy Violet, Sweet Violet and Early Dog Violet. Numerous bones of small mammals, such as this rabbit's skull, are seen in the woods at this time of year.

In the pond at the entrance to Rush Meadow were Sticklebacks and a great many Smooth Newts; also large Water Boatmen and a few Pond Skaters on the surface. A cock Reed Bunting flew out of the Sallow tree beside the pond as I arrived, and out on the meadow beyond were several Grey Squirrels feeding busily – I wondered on what?

Reed Bunting.

Coming back down the green road, I passed the only field of spring barley in the vicinity and found it covered with feeding birds: Rooks, Starlings, House Sparrows, a sizeable flock of Tree Sparrows, Chaffinches, Yellowhammers, Linnets and at least one pair of Siskins. I also watched through the hedge a pair of Brown Rats busily digging up barley plants and eating the grain. The larger of the two – the male? – was a proper old Samuel Whiskers, very plump, with one tattered ear. After a while they saw or winded me, and scampered off into a nearby culvert.

For the remainder of the month the weather was dry and bright with cool winds mainly from the north or north-east. The grass grew slowly and the hedges greened as Elder, Hawthorn and Dog Rose came into leaf. By the end of April the snowy Blackthorn blossom was fully out and the great mounds of golden Kingcups made a splendid show in the marsh and along the brookside, as did the Cowslips on Peticote and in the thicket glades. Other flowering plants on or around the edges of the

meadows during this period were Field Woodrush, White Dead-nettle, Ribwort Plantain, Garlic Mustard and, along the bridleway, Cow Parsley and Greater Stitchwort. The Cuckoo Pint produced its curious brown or purplish spikes, enclosed by narrow, leaf-like spathes, but any that were not already concealed by the rising tide of nettles and other coarse herbage had been nibbled off by creatures, possibly rabbits, obviously immune to its poison. The great Black Poplar tree also carried a mass of deep crimson catkins in its crown.

As the weather warmed, the Sticklebacks moved out of the deep water and the males took up breeding territories in the shallows.

The insects were slow to emerge: apart from the Peacocks, Commas and Brimstones, I saw only a few Small Tortoiseshell butterflies. Bumble-bees were chiefly Buff-tailed, and the round, furry Bee Fly, hovering with long proboscis extended, was a frequent sight in the last week of April.

The Snipe, unfortunately, did not stay to breed in the marsh, as in previous years, and I saw none after 25th April. On the same day I spotted the last Siskin of the year. Tawny Owls were nesting in the Spinney: I glimpsed one of them now and then, and in late evening visits heard the hooting of the male and the answering 'kiwik, kiwik' of the female. Several pairs of Stock Doves joined the numerous Wood Pigeons in the meadows, and I saw or heard the occasional Collared Turtle Dove near the farm. The Wrens, their call startlingly loud for such a tiny bird, were in fine voice and one evening I heard three singing at the same time from different points around Peticote; but for me the quintessential sound of late April, audible through every daylight hour, from every hedge, wood and thicket, was the lovely, cascading song of the Willow Warblers.

Opposite. Cowslip, Daisy and Field Woodrush (on the left) flower on the meadows in May. Ground Ivy (right) grows at the hedge-bottoms but spreads out into the meadows. Peacock butterflies, with wings expanded, enjoy the spring sunshine.

MAY

Pussy Willow going over, Kingcups and Blackthorn in flower and Lapwing displaying over the marsh in early May.

May was a rather cold and miserable month, the wind lingering obstinately in the east or north-east for much of the time. During the first few weeks hardly any rain fell, so that flowers on the drier ground began to wilt, and even the Bluebells in the woods hung their heads. As one bright, cold, cloudless day followed another, the meadow grass seemed reluctant to grow, but there was colour nonetheless on Peticote as the Cowslips mingled with the white patches of Common Mouse-ear Chickweed and the clear blue of Germander Speedwell. On Poplar and Rush the tiny, pale flowers of Thyme-leaved Speedwell commenced their long season, which was to last until October, and in the wetter parts of Peticote and Poplar little mauve puffs of Lady's Smock appeared. Other species that flowered on the meadows during May were Meadow Buttercup, Dandelion and, towards the end of the month, Red Clover, Black Medick and the very similar-looking Lesser Yellow Trefoil. Red Campion bloomed beside the hedges and in the woodland borders, and Bluebells crowded the thickets and hedge bottoms all along the green road.

Germander Speedwell.

On the evening of 10th May, after a sharp afternoon shower that left puddles in the road but did not affect the generally droughty conditions, I went down to the meadows and noticed a strong smell of fox around the badger setts in the thickets. Having spent some time in the marsh finding and identifying the three species of sedge that were then among the principal flowering plants – stands of Lesser Pond Sedge in the main bog areas, Hairy Sedge and Glaucous Sedge mixed with grasses around

the fringes – I continued towards the Spinney and was confronted by a large adult fox on the bridleway. We stood still and stared at each other for several seconds before the fox unhurriedly turned, leapt across the ditch into the Spinney and loped off into the undergrowth. I walked on slowly down Spinney and Rush Meadows, following the course of the brook. The Blackthorn bushes had nearly finished flowering, and still stretches of water were white with their fallen petals. Sticklebacks were everywhere in evidence, and I noticed the first Whirligig beetles of the season gyrating madly on the surface of one of the pools.

Previous page. The strange flowers of Cuckoo Pint,
also known as Lords-and-ladies or Jack-in-the-Pulpit,
are soon concealed by the rising tide of vegetation
around them. This gives them protection and allows
them to ripen their fruits.

Meadow Buttercup grows all over the meadows. Cuckoo flower, also known as Lady's Smock or Milkmaids, is confined to the wetter parts.

Coming back as dusk approached, I was standing by the brook and peering across it into the Spinney, hoping to catch another glimpse of my supposed Water Rail, when there was a rustle in the reeds just beyond the stream, and a Roe Deer suddenly sprang into view and immediately went bounding off through the Spinney, disappearing into the little plantation on the far side. It was a buck, with clean antlers, and I wondered if there was a doe lying up somewhere in the vicinity, either about to give birth, or guarding newborn fawns.

As I returned to my car, a Mistle Thrush was singing exuberantly from a tree at the edge of Brock's Pit.

A persistent light rain on 20th May gave the ground its first thorough soaking since the latter part of April. In the afternoon I had a long walk round all the meadows, the rain dripping from the peak of my cap, streaming off my oilskin coat and somehow managing to find its way inside my collar. Nevertheless, it was rather enjoyable, as a respite from the bitter north-easterly winds that had hitherto kept the month unseasonably cool. Fewer creatures than usual were abroad, but there were rabbits, as ever, on Peticote, and Starlings flying urgently to and fro with food for their clamorous young. I saw the first Turtle Doves of the season and the first Swifts, hawking low over Peticote and Poplar.

In the Blackthorn thickets a Blackcap was singing, and a pair of Greenfinches were feeding and uttering their wheezy calls among the bright yellow male catkins of a White Willow.

On East Meadow the hay crop, though somewhat stunted by the drought, was starting to thicken up, and Ryegrass, Meadow Fescue, Cocksfoot, Meadow Foxtail and Annual Meadow Grass were all in flower. On the other meadows the most prominent flowering grass was Sweet Vernal, the species that imparts to old meadow hay its sweetest scent. By this time most of the trees and hedgerow shrubs were in leaf, including the oaks, Alders and Black Poplars that are always among the last; only some of the Ashes, their flowering over, remained with leafless twigs. The Hawthorn blossomed and filled the air with its distinctive scent.

Throughout May, the attractive pale purple flowers of Ground Ivy formed large clumps beside the hedges, and in the thicket glades the deep blue spires of Bugle grew up among the grasses. Yellow Rocket flowered in some of the ditches, and beside the green road hedge, on

Peticote, I found two colonies of Hound's Tongue, a handsome and rather uncommon plant, related to Comfrey, with downy, grey-green leaves and numerous small, deep crimson flowers.

The large, yellow flowers of the Dandelion make a brave show in May, and might be more admired if they were less familiar or less unpopular with gardeners.

Towards the end of the month I saw the first House Martins feeding in the company of Swallows over Peticote Meadow. They nest every year under the eaves of the nearby fourteenth-century farmhouse, but the cold weather during May, and consequent shortage of insects, kept them busy finding food, and the process of nest-building and egg-laying was retarded. On 28th May I recorded the first Spotted Flycatcher and a Great Spotted Woodpecker which flew out of a dead Elm on East Meadow. A week or so earlier I had found a Willow Warbler's nest with six eggs in it suspended among briars and tangled vegetation about six inches above the ground, in the bridleway hedge on Spinney Meadow.

Above. The lovely, blue-flowered spikes of Bugle favour damp and shady spots and are often partly hidden by the dense vegetation around them.

Opposite. Hound's-tongue is one of the rarer plants found on the meadows. It grows in the shade of the green road hedge on Peticote.

The weather remained cool until the end of the month and butterflies were rather scarce, though Orange-tips, Peacocks and Brimstones appeared whenever the sun gave a little warmth.

Other insects included a mayfly (I think a Pond Olive) resting on a grass stem beside the Rush Meadow pond, and an alderfly in the marsh. *Empis tesselata*, a species of large dipteran or true fly, was sometimes abundant on May blossom, and in the rainwater puddles of the green road I often found wriggling, scarlet bloodworms which are the larval stage of Chironomid midges. A handsome shieldbug, *Eysarcoris fabricii*, with gold and coppery markings on its dorsal surface, was quite common on the leaves of Hedge Woundwort and White Dead-nettle.

Pipistrelle Bat.

JUNE

There was a gradual improvement in the weather during the first week of June, though it was not until the 9th that the first really perfect summer day came – very warm with a clear blue sky and light southerly breeze – marking the beginning of a period of good weather that was to last, with only very brief breaks, until the end of August. One such break occurred on 17th June, but I found much to record before that, spending long hours on the meadows, enjoying the balmy weather and reluctantly returning to my desk to write and paint

Pair of Lapwing.

Poplar Meadow had not been grazed in early June and now, on both sides of the brook, it was a sea of vivid yellow starred with white from the flowers of Creeping Buttercup and Daisy. These were by far the most plentiful of the meadow species throughout the month, for the East Meadow hay crop was disappointingly short of flowers and the open areas of Peticote, Spinney and Rush Meadows were close-cropped by the grazing ponies. Smooth Meadow Grass and Crested Dogstail were among the grasses flowering on all the meadows and at the west end of Poplar, against the hedge, a big patch of Chervil bloomed, as it did in the open parts of the green road and other bridleways, where it replaced the now seeding Cow Parsley. On Rush Meadow several plants of Hemlock appeared, but these, being highly poisonous, were pulled up in case the horses should be tempted to nibble them. My most exciting discovery

Opposite. A view looking down into the old sandpit, from the top of Brock's Pit Wood, in June.

was a single Southern Marsh Orchid at the west end of the thicket glades where Common Spotted Orchids were also growing, though the latter were still several weeks off flowering. It had a tall, many-flowered inflorescence, and I searched carefully through the marsh, and in all other likely spots, but failed to find another specimen. I did, however, find one nearly a fortnight later, growing in the Orchid bog. This is the specimen I have illustrated, rather smaller than the first one, which I drew *in situ*, crouching uncomfortably among the tall sedges and enveloped by a cloud of midges.

The brook still carried a good volume of water from the rains of winter and early spring, but the vegetation on its banks grew apace, and in places the flow could hardly be seen as beds of Water Cress and blue-flowered Brooklime spread across it. In the marsh Ragged Robin started to flower, clumps of False Fox Sedge appeared here and there, and beds of Marsh Horsetail developed, although the whorls of feathery branchlets had yet to expand.

Throughout the marsh area, particularly on the broad, sword-shaped Iris leaves, I found innumerable small Succineid snails of the species *Oxyloma pfeifferi*, whose elongated shells have only a few minute twists at the tip. I also came across the large Garden Snail, generally among ivied roots in the bridleways, and a whitish, mottled snail called *Monacha cantiana* that was widespread on tall vegetation. The smaller, hairy-shelled *Trichia hispida* was fairly common, but by far the most attractive species, with shells varying from clear yellow to salmon pink or cream with chocolate brown bands, was *Cepaea nemoralis*, which I also found quite frequently in the form of broken fragments around a Song Thrush's anvil-stone.

As I walked through the thicket glades, the scent from the bruised leaves of Water Mint rose up and mingled with the heavy perfume of the Hawthorn blossom. Common Forget-me-not, Welted Thistle, Cleavers and Bush Vetch flowered, and there was a great volume of bird-song,

Opposite. Common Spotted Orchids (left) are plentiful
among the sedges on the north side of the brook. In
other parts of the marsh and in the thicket glades they
occur more sparsely. Of the Southern Marsh Orchid
(right) I found only two specimens.

besides various call notes, scoldings and twitterings, from birds that were either nesting or hunting for food among the Blackthorns and other bushes. By this time the leaf coverage was so heavy that birds were much more frequently heard than seen, and usually I had to identify them by their song: Bullfinches, Linnets, Dunnocks, Great and Blue Tits, a pair of Coal Tits, Spotted Flycatchers, Willow Warblers and Whitethroats. Many of the resident birds, such as Blackbirds, Song Thrushes and Starlings, already had well grown youngsters out and about, and on 3rd June I came across a family party of seven Long-tailed Tits. It was the same day that I heard my first Cuckoo of the season from the meadows, although elsewhere I had been hearing Cuckoos on and off since 23rd April.

It is difficult to combine botanising and bird-watching, since one cannot simultaneously peer down at the ground and up into the trees and sky. I decided to concentrate either on flowers and insects (with an ear cocked for any unfamiliar bird-song) or, when the locality seemed right, on birds. On the evening of 9th June, I was strolling homewards and stopped by the Spinney to look back towards the setting sun. The light was golden and the air full of dancing insects and fluffy Sallow seeds floating down very slowly and sparkling in the sunlight. A small bat (probably a Pipistrelle) came out and flew back and forth half a dozen times above me; I pinpointed it with the glasses and saw it catch an insect before it vanished. As I stood gazing at this peaceful scene, I heard the drumming of a woodpecker from the Spinney and searched among the treetops with my glasses until I found it hammering away at a branch of an old and cankered Ash tree. It was a Lesser Spotted Woodpecker, a species that has increased considerably over the last twenty years. After watching it for a while, I wandered slowly through the wood and came upon several other birds including a pair of Willow Warblers, a Stock Dove, a Tree Sparrow and a Garden Warbler. The most conspicuous choristers now were Blackbirds, Song Thrushes and Chaffinches, with the cooing of Wood Pigeons as a constant background sound. Willow Warblers were still singing, but their song, so omnipresent in late April, was now drowned out by the general chorus.

*Opposite. The two most characteristic plants of the
brook are Water Cress (in foreground) and Brooklime.
The dragonfly is a male Broad-bodied Chaser.*

*Hop Trefoil (on left) and Black Medick (with bright
yellow flowers), White Clover and Red Clover are all
plants of the open meadowland. A male Orange-tip
butterfly feeds on a clover-head.*

A few days previously, on 7th June, I had walked with a couple of friends, one of them an experienced badger-watcher, all round the meadows and woods in search of badger setts. It was a windy day, sunny at first, then spitting with rain, and we had started with the setts in the bank on the south side of the Blackthorn thickets. A family of Badgers had been reared here the previous year, but now there was no sign of them, although we found ample evidence of foxes instead: tracks in the damp, sandy soil, droppings, pigeon carcases and pheasants' wings. After that we explored Brock's Pit which was already becoming something of a jungle with the undergrowth – consisting largely of Stinging Nettles – growing up fast. Near the centre of the wood we came across a series of setts that showed obvious signs of recent use, and soon established that Badgers were in residence. We found only one clear footprint – of an adult – but also badger hairs adhering to tree roots inside the holes, and several of the setts had sand and old bedding material raked back five or six yards from their mouths. We found no evidence – such as tracks or a play area – to indicate the presence of young Badgers.

Exploring the wood further, we came upon the stump of a dead elm tree at the head of the old sandpit, eight or nine feet high, which was covered all over and around its base with the handsome fungus *Pleurotus cornucopiae*, a species that has become a lot commoner in recent years because of spreading Dutch Elm disease.

Other fungi growing around this time on the meadows were the very delicate little *Bolbitius vitellinus*, whose young specimens have bright yellow caps and silky white stems, and *Panaeolus semiovatus*, a species that grows from horse dung.

The pond on Rush Meadow was still full of Smooth Newts, both adults and larvae. I scooped up several samples of water and pondweed in a jam jar, and found besides a great many small crustaceans (mainly *Cyclops* whose females are easily recognisable by the pairs of large egg-sacs that they carry around attached to their abdomens), a selection of small water beetles, mites and worms, and a number of Phantom Midge larvae; these transparent creatures, about half an inch long, which are generally suspended motionless and horizontal in the water, can move with such lightning speed that they seem to vanish entirely, only to reappear, motionless once again, perhaps an inch away. I also captured a dragonfly nymph and a large water beetle of the species *Acilius sulcatus* whose hind legs are adapted to form a pair of powerful paddles. I moved on reluctantly, realising that to make a full study of the pond's fauna could keep me busy for the rest of the summer, leaving little time for observing anything else. The surface of the pond was becoming obscured by the spread of Water Starwort and Lesser Duckweed and at its east end, growing partly on the mud and partly in the water, there was a mass of white-flowered Water Crowfoot. Two other plants that I noticed flowering at this time were the slender, gracefully curved Woodland Brome Grass – in the wetter and shadier parts of the bridleways – and the pink-flowered Herb Robert in a similar situation between the Spinney and Peticote Meadow.

Insects became more numerous, and in the thicket glades, especially, there was a constant hum from the nectar-sipping bees and flies. Among the most prominent insects were leafhoppers and froghoppers (particularly the large black and scarlet *Cercopis vulnerata*), various species of crane fly and the nymphs of Dark Bush-crickets which abounded in the marsh and could be found among lush vegetation all over the meadows. I never saw any grasshoppers on Lapwing Meadows, although on several small hay meadows near my house and even in my garden, they were present in greater numbers than I had seen them in any previous year. This absence was presumably due to the horses' close-cropping of the turf, the ungrazed areas being too lush for grasshoppers, though ideal for crickets.

Wherever there was tall vegetation in shady places, such as the edges of the bridleways, I would put up small, pale moths, most of them 'micros' which I did not attempt to identify, but one species that I did recognise, very common around this period, was the Silver-ground Carpet.

On 9th June I found a large hatch of Azure Damselflies in the marsh: lovely delicate little insects, the males with bright blue bodies banded with black. There was also a male Broad-bodied Chaser dragonfly, with a broad, powder-blue abdomen, hunting low over a pool in the Orchid bog, and later, on Rush, I was able to study the green, tawny and yellow female of the same species at close quarters, as it rested on a spray of Bramble.

Beetles, of all shapes and sizes, abounded, but by far the most

The massed pink and white flowers of Dog Rose make a glorious show in the hedgerows and thickets.

ubiquitous, now and throughout the whole summer, were the orange-red Soldier Beetles, especially conspicuous because they were usually exposed on the flower-heads of umbelliferous and other plants. I also came across a splendid blood-red Cardinal Beetle, of which there are only three British species. This one, with a red head, I identified as *Pyrochroa serraticornis*.

Butterflies became more and more abundant with the warm days, especially Green-veined Whites, Small Whites and Orange-tips. I saw occasional Brimstones and, on 9th June, the first Small Heaths and Large Whites – the latter a species that has become much less common in recent years.

In the brook the Sticklebacks were busy preparing to breed. On one occasion, early in the month, I lay on the bank above a shallow pool where three males were guarding their little domed nests which were placed in a triangle two to three feet apart. Whenever a female ventured among them, each male in turn would dart at her and try to drive her into his nest. If in any of these forays a male entered the territory of another, he would be smartly chased off. Each had a favourite lair near the nest where he would lie in wait, his pectoral fins gently fanning, occasionally approaching the nest to inspect it and give it a touch-up where necessary. A little way downstream, another male was building his nest, bringing small pieces of material in his mouth and then moulding them into the mud fabric of the nest by running his body over it with a strong vibrating motion. Some females, all big with spawn, were gathered in a bunch in a current of fast-flowing water upstream. Every now and then, one would sally forth to have a quick flirt. The males, when excited or angry, turned perceptibly brighter in colour, bluish-green on top and ruby-red underneath, especially around the gills. The object of the exercise was to get the female into the nest, where she would lay her eggs for the male to fertilise.

The only other fish species that I encountered in the brook was a Miller's Thumb (or Bullhead) which I disturbed one day as I was wading up a shallow, gravelly reach near the Spinney, turning up stones in search of leeches and caddis larvae. It emerged from the bottom with a

Opposite. Yellow Flag Iris forms an extensive bed in marshy ground on the south side of the brook.

puff of sand, moved a few yards very rapidly and vanished again, but its shape – all head and very little body – made its identity certain.

On 17th June, the fine weather was interrupted by a tremendous thunderstorm. The rain was torrential, flattening vegetation, causing floods and bringing tons of mud off the Sugar-beet fields to lie inches thick on the roads. Huge hailstones battered and shredded the flowers and vegetables in gardens all around the neighbourhood and even smashed greenhouses. A fierce wind accompanied the storm, ripping branches from trees and littering the meadows with leafy twigs of oak and Ash blown far out from the hedgerows.

The next morning started with a dense mist, but this gradually evaporated and the day became sunny and very warm. The break, despite its fury, had been brief, and placid weather was with us again.

I went away on holiday on 23rd June for three weeks, but during the last week before my departure there was plenty to record.

The Lapwing had been less conspicuous during the previous few weeks (although I saw a couple of birds around the marsh on most visits), but on the 18th they were displaying and very vocal again, still uttering their breeding calls. A Wall Brown butterfly was perched on the bank by the East Meadow gate (the only sighting I had of this species) and a Linnet sang melodiously from the hedge. Just inside the gate was an area that had been so poached and compacted by the horses' hooves during the winter that it had never grown any grass, but I found it covered now with Shepherd's Purse and the strongly scented Rayless Chamomile. In the meadow, where the hay crop was nearly ready for mowing, Yorkshire Fog and Timothy were two more grasses that had come into flower and among their stems I found Self-heal, with its tightly-clustered violet-blue flowers, and patches of White Clover starting to bloom.

I walked across to the ditch that runs out of Brock's Pit, and there I found Figwort, Water Figwort, Lesser Hairy Willow-herb and Hedge Woundwort all in flower, together with a single plant, over three feet tall, of what I thought at first to be the rare Rough Hawk's-beard, but which I later decided was probably an unusually large and prickly example of the much commoner Beaked Hawk's-beard. I went on to Brock's Pit where

Opposite. Ragged Robin grows all over the marsh,
where the snail Oxyloma pfeifferi *is also common.*

the undergrowth was now so tall and dense that I could hardly penetrate inside the wood, and then down again to Poplar Meadow. Everywhere the wild roses were in flower, their pink or white blooms cascading down out of the tall hedges and making a splendid show. I walked along the south side of the brook on Poplar, lingering in the central, and wettest, part of the meadow, where much of the sward was made up of Flote Grass and Hairy Sedge; here I also found Procumbent Marshwort (a creeping plant with small white flowers, sometimes known as Fool's Watercress), Jointed Rush and the tiny, aptly named Bristle Scirpus. In the middle of this area was a very small pool, only a few yards across, that was surrounded by Pink Water Speedwell. The common (blue-flowered) Water Speedwell was in bloom all along the edge of the nearby brook.

The next few days were all hot and sunny and I spent as much time as possible on the meadows. The marsh was particularly colourful, for the large bed of Yellow Flag was now fully out and mixed among the Irises were the pink flowers of Ragged Robin, while on the other side of the brook the pale lilac or occasionally white spikes of Common Spotted Orchid were beginning to spring up among the sedges, although some, in more exposed positions, had been nibbled off, presumably by the horses. Other flowering plants included Water Chickweed, Marsh Bedstraw and Marsh Thistle.

On the last visit to the meadows before my holiday, I walked through the marsh and experienced a strong sense of the pullulating life all around me: Turtle Doves crooned in the thickets; somewhere in the distance a Cuckoo called monotonously; Swallows and House Martins performed their aerial ballet over Peticote, and the songs of many different birds merged together and joined with the drone of flying insects to create an all-pervading volume of sound. I had only to look down at the rich variety of plants all around me to see that these, too, supported a seething mass of living creatures.

Among the many insects that I noted during those glorious June days were black and yellow Wasp Beetles, the large drone fly *Volucella bombylans*, a ruby-tail wasp *Chrysis ignita*, and numerous kinds of bee including Honey Bees, Small Garden, Buff-tailed and Large Red-tailed Humble Bees, Common Carder Bees and a Vestal Cuckoo Bee. One dragonfly flying about the marsh showed a broad, powder-blue abdomen and was almost certainly the Broad-bodied Chaser, though I never managed to get close to it while it was perched. The same day I found, resting on a nettle by the gate to Poplar Meadow, the loveliest, to my mind, of all the damselflies, a female Banded Demoiselle which has a thorax and abdomen of iridescent emerald green, turning gold towards the tail, and fulvous wings. The male, with broad indigo bands across the wings and a sapphire body, is equally magnificent, though I did not see one on the meadows. The species is more usually found, and often in abundance, beside slow-flowing rivers.

My holiday was spent in Scotland, the first two weeks fishing a small west coast spate river, the third sailing among the islands of the Inner Hebrides. Our fishing quarters were situated near the mouth of the river, where it joined a sea loch, with tall mountains on the northern side of the valley and smaller hills to the south. The habitats for wildlife, both plant and animal, were therefore very varied in our immediate vicinity, with tidal mudflats and saltings, freshwater marshes and wet meadows, hill meadows, natural woodland and high heather moorland interspersed with lochs. I found, in profusion, many of the plants, birds and insects that I had been recording on Lapwing Meadows, and a great deal more besides: on the first morning I found four species of orchid, two of which were new to me, and walked through a meadow full of Yellow Rattle, where two species of fritillary butterfly – both now extinct in Essex – were present in numbers that reminded me of Meadow Browns at home.

The richness and diversity of flora and fauna seemed, momentarily, to make a mockery of my efforts in recording the wildlife of a tiny green oasis amid the arable desert of East Anglia. Yet, in fact, it merely underlined the importance of preserving what little remains to us of that older, less intensively farmed, landscape that has largely, and (in view of the surpluses now being produced) unnecessarily, been destroyed. One of the great charms of this country is the variety of its landscape and ecology, which change so dramatically and so frequently from place to place. There were plants and animals to be found on Lapwing Meadows that were absent here in Scotland. Indeed, every wood, meadow and spinney, wherever situated and however unremarkable in appearance, is, in its association of species, to some extent unique, deserving, at least, some consideration before it is obliterated for ever.

JULY

Southern Hawker dragonfly.

I returned from Scotland in mid-July and visited the meadows again on a sultry, overcast day with showers developing in the afternoon and only occasional glimpses of the sun. I walked round East Meadow first, where most of the hay had been cut, baled and carted, though some, slower to dry in the shade of the tall hedgerows, still lay in the swath. Wisps of steam rose from it after a passing shower.

All the meadows had acquired a shaggier appearance since I had last seen them, the tall vegetation in the horses' dunging areas and beside the hedges having grown prodigiously. Much of it had been battered and knocked by heavy rains, and creeping plants such as Cleavers and White Bryony rioted among it and clawed up into the hedges. On Poplar, beyond the brook, the coarser vegetation had so encroached on the short turf that the area had been divided into three separate glades, joined only by narrow paths kept open by the horses. These jungles consisted mainly of Field Thistle and Spear Thistle, Broad-leaved, Curled and Red-veined Dock, Hogweed, Ragwort and Stinging Nettle, all now in flower; Nipplewort, Hedge Woundwort and Black Horehound grew along the hedgerows, and the attractive pink and white flowers of Lesser Bindweed spread out into the meadows.

Hedgehog running into cover.

The Buttercups and Daisies of the meadows had largely been replaced, particularly on Poplar, Spinney and Rush, by great drifts of purple-flowered Self-heal, mixed, very often, with White Clover. On Rush, just beyond the pond, I came upon a small patch – perhaps two dozen flower-heads – of the uncommon pink-flowered form of Self-heal, and a few days later I found some more only a few yards away.

Benjamin Perkins 1904.

The most westerly of the grassy glades over the brook on Poplar was a mass of Common Centaury, though on that first July visit the pretty coral-pink flowers, always sensitive to sunshine or the lack of it, were closed; and there I also found the yellow Smooth Hawk's-beard and Common Cat's-ear. A miniaturised form of Smooth Hawk's-beard, matching the close-cropped turf, was widespread all over Peticote, while taller specimens, together with the small, pink-flowered Cut-leaved and Dove's-foot Cranesbill, were growing beside the hedges and in the roughs. On Poplar I found a quantity of Toad Rush near the stream, growing among the grasses and small sedges.

Above. The purple flowers of Self-heal are found all over the meadows, but the rare pink-flowered form occurs only on Rush Meadow. Smooth Hawk's beard (with yellow flowers) and Lesser Bindweed are both abundant, as is the Meadow Brown butterfly.

Previous pages. Looking eastwards across Peticote Meadow in July.

In the thicket glades Meadowsweet was starting to flower, filling the air with that most evocative of high summer scents; the magenta flowers of Hardheads and (to a lesser extent) Greater Knapweed were scattered here and there on sunny banks, mixed with the narrow pale yellow spikes of Agrimony. Prickly Sowthistle, Yarrow and Great Plantain were also in flower, and climbing everywhere among the rank vegetation, sometimes to a height of four foot or more, was Yellow Meadow Vetchling. Flowering grasses included Couch Grass, Soft Brome and both Common and Creeping Bent.

As I strolled through the thicket glades, Wood Pigeons and an occasional Stock Dove would erupt with a great clatter of wings out of the Blackthorn bushes where their eggs were laid on meagre platforms of twigs; I wondered, as always, why they did not sit tight, hidden and protected as they were by the leaves and thorny branches of the bushes where I would never have suspected their presence had they not proclaimed it so noisily. Bumble-bees – mostly Large Red-tailed, Small Earth and Small Garden – were busy everywhere; and on the leaves of Water Mint there were clusters of small, round bronze-coloured beetles of the genus *Chrysolina*, which I continued to see throughout the summer. I spotted a Scorpion Fly and also several Soldier Flies – beautiful creatures that either hovered over the vegetation (causing me, at first, to mistake them for hover flies) or rested with wings folded over their backs. In the males, both abdomen and thorax shone like burnished brass, but the thorax of the females was bottle green with glints of purple.

As I came out of the thickets into the marsh, two Lapwing got up and flew off with plaintive cries, a Tawny Owl hooted from the Spinney and I was scolded by a family of Whitethroats from the Sallow bush in the Orchid bog. Meadowsweet was in flower here too, the creamy, scented flowers justifying its alternative name, Queen of the Meadows. Among the now fruiting Iris, tall plants of creamy-pink Hemp Agrimony had grown up and were starting to bloom, and the yellow and orange flowers of Marsh Bird's-foot Trefoil added touches of bright colour to the scene. Also in flower here and there were Hard and Soft Rush, Lesser Stitchwort, Reed Canary Grass and Great and Lesser Hairy Willow-herb, while across the brook, in the Orchid bog, I found a few Orchids still flowering as well as Tufted Vetch and Square-stalked St John's Wort.

The marsh vegetation teemed with spiders of many different kinds,

*Flower-heads of Black Horehound; I came across the
unusual white-flowered form growing beside the hedge
on Spinney Meadow.*

including small jumping spiders which, as their name implies, capture their prey by stalking and springing upon it, and wolf spiders, another group whose members hunt their victims instead of lying in wait beside a web; some of the female wolf spiders carried a cluster of baby spiders on their backs. Another very common hunting spider, *Pisaura mirabilis*, with an elongated, hairy body, builds tent-like webs to protect its cocoons, and these I found all over the marsh. Among the builders of orb webs, the most prominent species was *Nuctenea cornuta*, a large and handsome spider whose ivory-coloured abdomen has bold, dark brown markings.

On Spinney Meadow, Common Mallow was in flower by the green road hedge and the first white trumpets of Great Bindweed showed here and there among the tangle of bushes and creepers beside the brook. A Lesser Spotted Woodpecker flew up out of a large Sallow bush and into the top of an Ash tree in the Spinney, where I got a good view of it through glasses, and I surprised a Moorhen on the brook with a brood of fluffy, sooty-black chicks which took cover by diving under the water. Near by, feeding very openly on the leaves of Water Figwort, I found a number of caterpillars of the Mullein Shark moth, doubtless relying, for protection from predators, on their vivid colouring – white with yellow bands and black spots. Later in the month I saw others on the opposite side of the meadow, feeding on the leaves of Common Mullein. Further down Spinney Meadow I came across an oddity in the shape of a small patch of Creeping Buttercup, all with double flowers.

The pond was considerably shrunken, its surface almost entirely obscured by beds of Water Plantain at one end and Branched Bur-reed at the other, with Lesser Duckweed covering most of the open water in between. Around the edge of the pond were Celery-leaved Crowfoot and Creeping Jenny, with its pairs of bright yellow flowers. Maida, my black Labrador bitch, sniffing under a thorn bush near by, discovered a hedgehog which rolled itself up while being examined, but soon scuttled off, burying itself beneath the debris in the hedge bottom.

After walking to the end of Rush, I returned by the green road. Black Bryony, Traveller's Joy, Woody Nightshade and Bramble were among the many species flowering in the hedgerow, with Field Poppy, Fat-hen, Red and White Campion and Scentless Mayweed on the open banks.

The next day was blustery with scudding clouds, brief showers and fitful sunshine, but most of the remaining days of July were dry and very warm. I spent much time on the meadows, wandering through the flower-scented glades or standing for long periods in the marsh while damselflies (Blue-tailed now, as well as Azure) and butterflies fluttered past, and Wood Pigeons cooed endlessly from the Spinney, thickets and hedgerow trees 'take *two* coos, Taffy'. Sometimes I sat on the bank of the brook while Maida wallowed, hippopotamus-like, in the cool water, only her head and back exposed, and sometimes I lay on the dry meadow grass watching the puffs of cumulus cloud drift slowly by, and the Swallows and House Martins looping and wheeling high above me in their never-ending search for insects to feed their young. Occasionally a Skylark would mount up into the cobalt-blue sky from a neighbouring cornfield and deliver its ecstatic song for a few minutes, before gliding down to earth again, but the volume of bird-song was now far less than in June. Song Thrushes, Chaffinches and Wrens still indulged in occasional bursts of song but the time was approaching when almost the only regular songster would be the Yellowhammer, his oft-repeated 'little-bit-of-bread-and-no-cheese' being as much the essential sound of harvest time and the dog days of high summer as the Cuckoo's call is of the spring. It was always a struggle (and sometimes I lost it) to drag myself away from the meadows and return to my desk and paint box during those delicious summer days.

Butterflies throve and multiplied in the hot weather. I saw Small Tortoiseshells throughout the month and Green-veined Whites up to the third week. Small Whites were not very plentiful and I noticed only one Large White, but Meadow Browns were very abundant both on the marsh vegetation and on thistle flowers in the glades, often in the company of Small Tortoiseshells and Commas. In the marsh, there were large numbers of Small Skippers from mid-July onwards, but fewer Large Skippers and for a shorter period. I saw my first Gatekeeper on the 21st and increasingly from then on, with peak numbers during August. My most exciting day for butterflies, however, was 28th July. In the morning, as I sat on my lawn, a White-letter Hairstreak settled on the grass a yard

Opposite. Hedge Woundwort has downy leaves which can be used to staunch bleeding. A Small Garden Humble Bee feeds on its flowers.

or two away; this pleased me, for although I see this small butterfly most years I am always afraid that it will be for the last time, since its larval food-plant is elm and its fortunes are therefore dependent on the continued spread of Dutch Elm disease. Had there been any mature elms still alive on the meadows, this species would surely have been there. That afternoon, walking beside the green road hedge on Rush, I happened to look up and noticed a small, dark butterfly flying among the upper branches of one of the many fine oaks that line the hedge. It disappeared, but five minutes later I saw two more chasing each other around the top of the tree. It took me half an hour or more, lying on my back in the meadow and training my binoculars towards the leafy crown of the tree, to confirm that they were, as I had suspected, Purple Hairstreaks. I managed to pinpoint one, when it settled on a leaf, and saw clearly the glint of purple on the dark uppersides of its spread wings. Although I remained watching them for nearly an hour, I never saw one come within twenty feet of the ground, a characteristic of the species that makes them a difficult quarry for the collector.

On 19th July, I saw my first Southern Hawker Dragonfly of the summer. This is a very large dragonfly with intricate patterns of green, yellow, chocolate brown and blue on its abdomen, and I was to see it frequently, on all the meadows, until the beginning of October. Other very common insects towards the end of the month included hover flies, green bottles, earwigs and green lacewings; and from nettle beds in the bridleways I would often put up plume moths and other moth species including Common Wainscot, Common Footman and, once, a Coxcomb Prominent.

Among the less welcome types of insect were biting midges and thunderflies (or thrips), the latter so numerous on some hot and sultry days that I was continually wiping them from my face and scratching at my hair and beard where they got trapped in their hundreds and itched abominably! Worst of all, however, were the clegs, which were particularly bad around the pond, pouncing on me each time I skirted it on the way to Rush Meadow, and delivering painful bites if I was not quick enough to locate them. No doubt they lurked there for the horses that paid regular visits to the pond in order to drink, but other prey was just as welcome; they would arrive noiselessly, often landing on a clothed portion of the anatomy, and then crawling towards the nearest piece of

Small Copper butterflies feeding on the flower-heads
of Hemp Agrimony, which grows in the marsh.

exposed flesh such as the neck or an arm, before biting. I managed to pick up one which I had swatted just in time and took it home for examination. It was a female *Haemotopota pluvialis* (the males live, not on blood, but on nectar), and what appeared in the field to be a dull, hairy, greyish fly, turned out, under the lens, to have features of considerable beauty: intricately decorated wings and large, iridescent eyes patterned with swirling, dark brown arabesques.

Throughout the latter days of July there was always the drone of combines from the surrounding cornfields, as the winter barley crop was harvested; and sometimes a column of smoke on the horizon, or smuts borne on the breeze, would indicate that stubble burning was in progress. Against this background it seemed strange to hear the song – so redolent of spring – of a Chiffchaff coming from Brock's Pit, as I did on several days towards the end of this month.

Plants that flowered, or that I now noticed in flower for the first time, included Water Mint and the tiny white, purple-centred flowers of Gipsywort in the marsh; Burdock in the thickets and other areas of rough herbage; the pinkish-mauve Field Scabious, and Wild Basil with its pink flowers emerging from cushions of numerous green calyces, beside the green road hedge on Peticote; Herb Bennet, with small yellow flowers, in the Spinney; and the handsome yellow Perforate St John's Wort (distinguished from related species by tiny pellucid dots on the leaves) on Rush. Beside the brook, and in the dunging areas on Poplar and Peticote, large colonies of Red Bartsia came into flower. This is a common enough plant, but not one that I had previously associated with meadowland; here I often saw it in company with Centaury, Smooth Hawk's-beard and Lesser Bindweed.

AUGUST

Overleaf. The thicket glades in August with yellow and mauve flowers of Fleabane and
Water Mint dominating the scene.

Benjamin
Perkins
1984.

The Green Woodpecker's call is supposed to presage rain. True or not, I heard one call as it flew over East Meadow on 1st August and, sure enough, I awoke next morning to a fine steady downpour and the accompanying steamy, aromatic smell that is exhaled by parched earth and vegetation after a good wetting. Though the weather remained warm, there were intermittent showers over the next few days which freshened up the grasses and other flowering plants on the meadows, oxygenated the stagnant lagoons which were all that remained of the brook in its upper reaches, and encouraged the oaks to put forth lammas shoots whose delicate pale green or orange-crimson leaves were in sharp contrast to the black and leathery first-generation leaves. Best of all, on Peticote Meadow, the effect of the rain on the warm earth was to produce a splendid crop of Field Mushrooms. All the dry, south-facing slopes of the meadow were covered with overlapping rings of dark green grass from which the mushrooms grew in their hundreds, and for about a week I enjoyed their incomparable flavour each morning with my bacon and eggs.

Apart from some thunderstorms around the middle of the month, the remainder of August, though sometimes muggy and overcast, was uniformly warm. The occasional rains were sufficient to ensure a profusion of flowers and the warmth encouraged insects of all kinds.

Ever since June, wherever the vegetation was lush, and especially in the marsh and glades, I had noticed large numbers of Dark Bush-cricket nymphs. When they were in their final instars (stages between moults) towards the end of July, I had only to part the vegetation to see sometimes as many as a dozen perched on leaves and stems. If approached with caution, they were not difficult to catch, and I noticed that many of them had bright green bellies. On the first day of August I was surprised to find that they had all vanished, as if by magic. I hunted in all the usual places and could find not a single specimen. Presumably they had gone down to ground level in order to slough their last nymphal skins, but it seemed odd that they should all have done so simultaneously. During the next few days they began to reappear as adults (green

Opposite. New growth, known as 'lammas shoots',
appears on oaks (as well as other trees) in July and
August, and is often very colourful. Lammas Day is
August 1st.

undersides now replaced by yellow) and soon they were as numerous as ever, though more dispersed and far more difficult to approach; instead of hopping to a neighbouring leaf they would drop towards the ground when disturbed, disappearing among the tangles of grass and moss. However, their presence was now advertised by the continuous 'singing' of the males, a sound produced by rubbing together toothed plates at the base of the wings, unlike the grasshoppers whose stridulatory organs are on their hind legs. Besides the Dark Bush-crickets, I also came across an Oak Bush-cricket – a smaller, bright green insect with long wings – which dropped on to my shoulder one day as I was walking down the green road; and I found two Speckled Bush-crickets – also green but with rudimentary wings – on Bramble leaves on Rush Meadow.

Two species of dragonfly made their appearance in the early part of the month: the large Brown Hawker, easily distinguished from the Southern Hawker by its yellowish-brown wings, and the much smaller Common Darter whose females have ochre-coloured bodies while the males are a dull shade of scarlet. The latter species was abundant, and continued so until the end of the summer. I would often come across one sunning itself on a hedgerow or pond-side plant, its wings spread out (a feature that distinguishes dragonflies from damselflies, which fold their wings over their backs) and then turned until the wing surfaces were in a vertical plane. On one occasion, in the thicket glades, I saw a Southern Hawker catch a small moth on the wing, and watched from a yard away as it settled on a nettle leaf and ate it, with clearly audible crunching sounds.

On that first August visit, I was walking through the Iris bog when I put up a hen Pheasant almost at my feet; she flew only a few yards with a squeak, a flick of the wings and a curious twisting motion, as if some hidden arm had thrown her into the air. I stood still, and parting the herbage just in front of me, exposed seven or eight fluffy, newly-hatched chicks. I backed away slowly and retraced my steps through the marsh, confident that the mother would soon return to her family. Near by, where the brook runs out of the Spinney through a culvert beneath the bridleway, there was a long, pond-like stretch of deep water which never dried up through the summer, even though there were completely dry

*Opposite. The handsome magenta flowers and
seed-heads of Spear Thistle.*

stretches higher up. A certain amount of water, no doubt, always seeped into it from the Spinney, and at its lower end it was dammed by a wall of mud thrown up by the horses where they habitually forded the brook, by branches and by other rubbish that had become lodged there. A Kingfisher was perched on a branch of Crack Willow above this pool, and I watched it for a moment or two through a screen of reeds before it saw me and flashed away, like a blue flame, among the dark Alders.

*Male and female Speckled Bush-crickets on Bramble
leaves.*

Passing through the Spinney, I disturbed a young Tawny Owl which flew up into an Ivy-covered Ash tree where it was immediately mobbed by a pair of Chaffinches and other small birds, and on Spinney Meadow I surprised a family party of half a dozen Goldfinches feeding on thistle heads. Beside the green road hedge I found a clump of Black Horehound with pure white flowers instead of its usual purplish ones, and on Bramble flowers close by, the first Holly Blue butterfly of the season.

I had picked some flowers in the marsh, and when I got home and put them in water I noticed that I had brought back with them a beautiful, small, pale yellow spider with long, delicate legs and various black dots and stripes on its abdomen. It was *Enoplognatha ovata*, and it had come complete with the round, silken, bluish-green cocoon that contained its eggs. The spider hangs this cocoon by a gossamer thread from a stem or flower-head and guards it carefully, frequently moving it from one place to another, using one of its hind pair of legs to propel it around and when at rest crouching over it and holding it with its front legs. This requires considerable dexterity, all the more since my specimen had the two middle legs on its left side missing – possibly lost in moulting, as sometimes happens. Next day it was still on the bunch of flowers and I returned it, cocoon and all, to the marsh. Later in the month I found another specimen of the same species, this time with bright red markings on a creamy background, guarding its cocoon in a silken shelter that it had formed within the curl of a leaf.

Another attractive small spider, which I found within the trumpet-shaped corolla of a Great Bindweed flower, was the crab spider *Misumena vatia*. Its colour, a very pale bluish-grey, with legs like slender tubes of porcelain, exactly matched the shadows on the white petals of the flower where it lurked, waiting for a suitable insect in search of pollen to approach within the grasp of its long, outstretched legs. The crab spiders (Thomisidae), despite their small size and delicate appearance, are armed with a very potent poison, and can capture and quickly kill insects very much larger than themselves. The name 'crab spider' refers to the crab-like way that they position their legs, and the fact that they are able, like crabs, to move sideways.

Flowers that I recorded during the month included Teasel and Yellow Melilot in the thicket glades, Purple Loosestrife by the brook, the tall, pinkish-white Wild Angelica (which grew also in the Spinney), Fleabane and Water Mint in the marsh. The latter two species also grew in great profusion in the glades, and the combination of the yellow Fleabane flowers with the pale mauve flowers of Water Mint was a superb sight throughout August and through much of September.

In the poplar glades tall plants of Prickly Lettuce came into flower, while the most easterly of the glades was almost entirely overgrown by Ragwort whose broad, golden-yellow flower-heads (though unloved by farmers) made a handsome show. Towards the middle of the month I began to notice, in the thicket glades, around the pond and elsewhere, plants of Hoary Ragwort, which differs from the common species in having more acutely lobed leaves with cottony undersides.

On Rush Meadow, I found several patches of the sweetly-scented, frothy yellow flowers of Lady's Bedstraw, and around the rainwater flashes Redshank and Red Goosefoot. The large yellow flowers of Corn Sowthistle were prominent near the pond and in several of the roughs, and clumps of pinkish-white Alsike Clover were dotted about the meadow.

Along the green road and the bridleways I found a number of common plants such as Mugwort, Creeping Cinquefoil, Hedge Parsley, Hedge Mustard, Groundsel, Scarlet Pimpernel and Common Knotgrass; but pride of place beside the green road and also along the hedge on Poplar Meadow belonged, undoubtedly, to the tall clumps of Nettle-leaved Bellflower, adorned with numerous large, bell-shaped, bright purple flowers.

On Peticote Meadow I found Hop Trefoil and also, near the Orchid bog, a few plants of Common Bird's-foot Trefoil. The latter interested me because it is (with Rest-harrow, which does not occur on the meadows) the principal larval food-plant of the Common Blue butterfly, which I recorded for the first time on 12th August and saw increasingly throughout the rest of the month and well into September. Yet the Bird's-foot Trefoil occurred so sparsely that I had hardly hoped to see any Common Blues. Marsh Bird's-foot Trefoil, however, was abundant in the area and I assume, though the books I consulted did not confirm it, that this was an acceptable alternative.

Butterflies, throughout August, were even more plentiful than they had been in July. Peacocks, Small Whites, Small Tortoiseshells and

Opposite. The tall and handsome Nettle-leaved
Bellflower – a wild relation of Canterbury Bells –
grows in shady places beside the green road and in the
hedge on Poplar.

Meadow Browns were always to be seen, and Gatekeepers, on peak days, must have been numbered in thousands rather than hundreds, although they started to get fewer towards the end of the month, and had virtually disappeared by the beginning of September. On 9th August I recorded eleven species which included, besides those just mentioned, Small Skippers, Large and Green-veined Whites, Commas, Brimstones and Holly Blues. The last, generally in ones and twos, fluttered around the hedgerows on Rush and Spinney Meadows, where Ivy, whose flower-buds form the larval food of the summer brood, grew on most of the trees; the spring butterflies lay their eggs on the flower-buds of Holly, which does not occur anywhere around the meadows. Common Blues, from 12th August, were usually about in the marsh area, and on the 17th, also in the marsh, I recorded the first Small Copper. These very attractive little butterflies, with their brown-spotted, burnished copper wings, are fiercely territorial and I would often find them occupying precisely the same small patch – beside the marsh, near the pond and half way down Rush Meadow – on each visit. They seemed to favour the flowers of Fleabane and if another small butterfly – copper or blue – approached, it would invariably fly up to intercept the intruder, and an aerial dog-fight would ensue.

Besides the butterflies themselves, I frequently saw colonies of Peacock or Small Tortoiseshell caterpillars, avidly feeding on the leaves of Stinging Nettles; and on 12th August, I came across a caterpillar of the Muslin Ermine moth – one of those hairy brown caterpillars that are generally referred to as 'woolly bears' – crawling across the ground by the East Meadow gate. Moths in general, being for the most part nocturnal, I did not record in any number, but occasionally I would notice one on a tree or a fence post, or flush it from its resting place among the wayside herbage in the bridleways; such specimens included the Canary-shouldered Thorn, Angle Shades, Copper Underwing, Plain Golden Y

Opposite. Flowers of high summer: left to right
Common Bird's-foot Trefoil, Fleabane, Purple
Loosestrife, Great Knapweed, Red Bartsia, Field
Scabious, Red-veined Dock, Meadow Sweet and
Yarrow, with Common Blue, Small Tortoiseshell and
Holly Blue butterflies and Seven-spot Ladybird beetle.

and the lovely Peach-blossom moth whose brown forewings are decorated with splashes of pale pink. Mother-of-Pearl moths were very common towards the end of August, fluttering around the Horehound and Woundwort in the hedge bottoms, and from mid-August until the summer's end, on all the meadows, I was continuously putting up Silver Y moths – a day-flying, migrant species, some of which reputedly come from as far away as North Africa.

On 17th August I came across a Lesser Stag Beetle in the grass on Poplar; this is a species that seems to be considerably more common than the large Stag Beetle whose splendid male, with his antler-like mandibles, I have seen only once in this vicinity. Beside the brook, on the same day, I noticed another of the large drone flies, this time *Volucella pelluscens*, whose black abdomen is encircled by a broad, pearly, translucent band.

Ladybird beetles were all over the meadows, in response, no doubt, to the increased numbers of aphids. Most were Seven-spot, followed by Two-spot and Twenty-two-spot Ladybirds.

A species of true bug that was now very prevalent, particularly in the thicket glades, was *Deraeocoris ruber*, the females red-brown and the males almost black, both sexes having a conspicuous red spot on either side of the abdomen. I also found the large and handsome Pied Shieldbug on Black Horehound beside the green road. The bugs (order Hemiptera) are for some reason much less familiar to the average person than, say, beetles or flies, although equally common. In addition to the typical species, such as those just mentioned, they include aquatic species such as Water Boatmen and Pond Skaters, parasites such as the Bed Bug and (in a separate section) the cicadas and leafhoppers.

The flowers of Water Mint attracted a great many Honey Bees, some dull and blackish, others with the forward part of the abdomen reddish-brown and the hinder part dark brown with well defined whitish bands. Many were drones, carrying no pollen and intent only on gathering nectar, but some (particularly on Fleabane) were carrying

Opposite. Ripening fruits of Cuckoo Pint appear in the hedge bottoms in August. The snails, both common species in the hedgerows surrounding the meadows, are Monacha cantiana *(left) and* Cepaea nemoralis.

bundles of deep orange pollen. Among the bees were several hover flies that were obvious bee-mimics. Water Figwort, a large bed of which grew beside the brook on Poplar, provided the favourite food for Common Wasps, presumably because its short reddish-purple flowers gave easy access to the nectaries – important for wasps which lack the long proboscises of bees and butterflies. I also saw quite a few Hornets, either zooming past me on their way to and from their nests, or on Ash saplings in the green road hedge where they were collecting bark to pulp for the construction or repair of their paper cells. Had I not seen them at this work, I would have been mystified by the large bare patches on the Ash stems which bore more resemblance to the damage done, nearer ground level, by Hares or rabbits. I would have been inclined to blame voles for it, and would certainly not have suspected any insect.

Grass Snake slipping into
the brook.

On 9th August, walking along the bridleway between Peticote and the Spinney, I surprised the only Grass Snake that I saw on the meadows during the whole summer. It was about two foot in length, and having crossed the path in front of me, it went winding and slithering down the bank towards the brook and disappeared among the tangle of reeds and nettles near the culvert. Moments later it reappeared, swimming across the brook, and finally vanished under the roots of a fallen willow, some five or six yards downstream.

The brook, as I have mentioned, was very low by this time, the pools below the Spinney being almost stagnant and connected to one another by the merest trickle of water. The Sticklebacks had retreated to the deepest pools, where their numbers were now augmented by shoals of minuscule young fry, but the most conspicuous creatures wherever there was a stretch of open water, were the freshwater shrimps, curious little animals (crustaceans but not, in fact, true shrimps) which have the unusual feature of swimming on their sides. Often I would see them swimming in couples, the male clutching the female to his underside.

On almost every occasion that I found myself on the meadows at dusk during those hot summer days, I would see bats patrolling up and down under the eaves of the woods or alongside the hedgerow trees. They were small, and almost certainly Pipistrelles, but on one occasion, early in the month, two very large bats passed high overhead and away out of sight, which were probably Noctules.

Seagulls fly continuously over the meadows throughout the year, except in the breeding season. Almost all are Black-headed Gulls, and on 12th August I was on Rush Meadow watching half a dozen of these on the soar, their graceful bodies immaculately white against the vivid blue of the sky, when I caught sight of what I thought at first to be two more, flying purposefully in a northerly direction. Something about their flight action caught my attention and turning my glasses towards them I noted their forked tails, black caps and pointed scarlet bills, and realised that they were terns. Presumably they were Common Terns, though the much less likely Arctic Tern is indistinguishable in flight.

On 20th August, standing by the brook where it runs through the marsh and facing the green road hedge, I had a ringside view through

Hunting Stoat.

binoculars of a Stoat hunting and catching a three-quarter-grown rabbit. The rabbit ran from the gate to a patch of rough grass some twenty yards out in the meadow, with the Stoat in pursuit, doubled back towards the hedge and out again to the rough, continuing to scamper madly to and fro. The Stoat would vanish momentarily or make off in the opposite direction, but seemed always to know exactly where the rabbit was, and to be thoroughly in control of the situation, whereas the rabbit was obviously in a state of dithering terror. Eventually the Stoat followed its victim into the rough. The rabbit ran out, squealing desperately, in a last bid for safety, and was caught just as it reached the hedge. For a minute both animals vanished. The Stoat then reappeared, grasping the rabbit by the nape of the neck and dragging it along the ground towards the gate, some ten yards away. It must have been heavy, for the Stoat was forced three times to put it down and rest, before finally pulling it into the hedge beside the gate post.

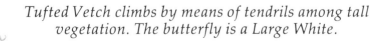

Tufted Vetch climbs by means of tendrils among tall vegetation. The butterfly is a Large White.

SEPTEMBER

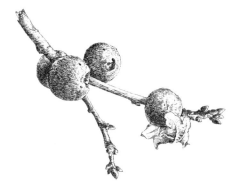

Overleaf. The Orchid bog in September, looking north-east, with House Martins overhead and a Heron picking its way through the grass tussocks.

The first day of September was almost the last of the real summer weather. It was very warm and the sky, at its zenith, was a deep ultramarine blue against which floated great, puffed-up, whipped-cream dollops of cloud with dazzling white crests and smoky, purplish-grey shadows. I walked round all the meadows, with Maida lagging unenthusiastically behind me, eager only for those moments when I stopped long enough for her to submerge herself in the brook. Everything had a tired, rather tattered, end-of-summer look, with brown seed-heads in place of flowers, leaves disfigured by caterpillars, patches of grass scorched brown by the heat and thistledown everywhere, floating through the air in clusters and adhering to the bushes. Yet there was still a lot of colour, particularly in the thicket glades where Fleabanc mingled with Water Mint and Ragwort. Butterflies were out in force, with Peacocks, Small Tortoiseshells, Small Whites and Meadow Browns all in good numbers. I also saw one very frayed Large White, several Small Coppers and more Common Blues than I had yet seen on any single day.

When I reached the marsh I was greeted as usual by the scolding 'tac, tac, tac' calls of the Whitethroats and as I walked on into the Iris bog, a Hare got up and went bounding away, through the hedge and over the wheat stubble beyond. I found its form and was bending down to feel with my hand the warmth left by its body on the compressed grass, when I spotted a superb Painted Lady butterfly on a leaf of Water Mint only a yard or two away. It was resting head downwards with wings spread in full sunlight, and obligingly stayed there while I sketched and photographed it. Later that day, when I called at the farmhouse on my way home, I saw another one, on a Russian Vine. These were the only two Painted Ladies that I saw that summer, and since it was a poor year for migrant

Painted Lady butterfly on a
Water Mint flower.

Benjamin Perkins 1984

butterflies – I had yet to see my first Red Admiral – I considered myself lucky to have seen any.

From the marsh I went on into the Spinney, where there was a Chiffchaff singing, and thence towards Rush Meadow. Beside the pond I came across a cluster of the large, hairy, black and yellow caterpillars of the Buff-tip moth, feeding voraciously on the leaves of a small Sallow bush. They had already completely denuded several branches. Goldfinches, Linnets and other seed-eating birds were feeding everywhere on the seeding thistle-heads and on Rush I noticed a Marsh or Willow Tit (the two are very hard to separate in the field except by their voices), flying into the hedge by the brook. Later I saw them feeding on thistles, delicately picking out one seed at a time and flying to the hedge before eating it. The field to the south of Rush was being ploughed and there was a continuous mewing sound of Lapwing as they fed, together with Black-headed Gulls, behind the plough. Walking back down the meadow, I saw several plants of yellow-flowered Bristly Ox-tongue – I must have passed them by on former occasions, assuming them to be Sowthistles. There were still many bumble bees about; I noticed a Red-shanked Carder Bee and also found a moribund Buff-tailed Humble Bee which was infested with large yellowish mites.

Twenty-four hours later the weather broke with a thunderstorm and a good heavy rain, and there followed a period of mainly rather cold, northerly winds, showers and intermittent sunshine as well as more thunderstorms, which lasted until 12th September. The next three or four days were sunny and breezy and I made several visits to the meadows, noting a lot of Southern Hawker and Common Darter dragonflies, plenty of Brimstones and at last, on the 13th, the first two Red Admirals of the season, feeding with Commas in the thicket glades. Swallows and House Martins were busy hawking over the meadows, feeding up now for the long journey to their winter quarters in southern Africa. I began to put up Snipe again as I walked beside the brook, the first since early spring, and on one early morning visit I surprised a Heron in the Orchid bog which rose up with a harsh cry, and flew off with ponderous wing beats.

Opposite. Looking down Rush Meadow through a
screen of Old Man's Beard and Bramble, on which a
Red Admiral butterfly is sunning itself.

Hoary Ragwort (lower left) and Common Ragwort.
Their bright yellow flowers make a pleasing sight,
although to farmers they are troublesome weeds.
The butterfly is a male Brimstone.

On 16th September, a soft, mild, greyish day, the willows were already dropping yellow leaves and on Poplar, Peticote and Spinney Meadows a second crop of Field Mushrooms had come up. Grey Squirrels were busy in the hedgerows, where the Hazel bushes were carrying an unusually heavy crop of nuts. I stood for some time by the hedge on Poplar, watching a Short-tailed Vole as it made repeated forays along the branches of an Elder, returning each time to the shelter of the Ivy-covered trunk. In the Poplar glades a party of some half-dozen Mistle Thrushes were feeding in the tops of the tall bushes and as I walked through the Blackthorn thickets a flock of well over a hundred Lapwing flew overhead. I noticed a lot of harvestmen, those rather primitive arachnids which, with their tiny bodies and enormously long legs, resemble a truncated Daddy-long-legs. Most of those I saw belonged to the species *Leiobunum rotundum*, which has a reddish-brown body and black legs.

*Field Mushrooms on Spinney Meadow among fallen
leaves of Crack Willow.*

On Spinney I stopped to pick some mushrooms before continuing into Rush. It was very still, the silence broken only by the twittering of birds in the hedgerows and the cooing of Wood Pigeons. No sound of traffic or any human activity reached me, and I lingered awhile, enjoying the unusual sensation.

In walking the meadows and attempting to record as much as possible of the wildlife there, two ploys had proved particularly productive. One was to choose a favourite spot, such as a part of the Iris bog where there was tall vegetation but where I still had a good all-round view, and to remain perfectly still for quite long periods. If I could, as it were, imagine myself to be a Sallow bush, it was surprising how often creatures would accept me as such and go about their business uninterruptedly. The other was to approach each new vista that opened up during the walk with the greatest care and circumspection, in the hope of glimpsing something of interest before being seen myself. If you walk boldly through a gateway and then put up your binoculars and start to survey the scene before you, it is ten to one that any birds or other sharp-sighted animals in the vicinity will have spotted you first and made a speedy getaway; you may get a fleeting glimpse of something flying away or disappearing into a thicket, but nothing you can identify with certainty – and that is very frustrating. As I proceeded from Spinney to Rush, therefore, I did so with great caution, peering first through a gap in the hedge from which I could see most of the meadow. I was rewarded by the sight of a small, dark wading bird – not, I quickly realised, a Snipe – which was dabbing with its beak at the muddy edge of the largest flash (again full of water) just beyond the pond. As it turned away, I saw its white rump and knew it for a Green Sandpiper; presently, when I went through into Rush Meadow and put it up, it flew off with a series of jinks, like a Snipe, but uttered a call 'wheet, wheet, wheet' very unlike the Snipe's harsh 'scaap', then rose high and circled round in a wide arc before flying off towards the south-west.

Besides the Bristly Ox-tongue, I recorded only four new flowering species during September. I found Grey (or Procumbent) Speedwell on East Meadow, a clump of Dyer's Rocket on Rush, quite a large stand of Pepper Mint on one of the tracks through Brock's Pit and, after forcing an entry into the smallest and most easterly of the thicket glades, which had been cut off by a wall of nettles, thorns and thistles since July, I

Buff-tip moth caterpillars
stripping a Sallow bush.

discovered a dozen or so plants of Devil's Bit Scabious. Fungi, on the other hand, were on the increase: Horse Mushrooms came up on Poplar, Spinney and in the thicket glades, Shaggy Ink Caps in the Poplar glades, and Shaggy Parasol Mushrooms under the Blackthorns in the thickets and in Brock's Pit. On most of the meadows there were rings of Fairy Ring Champignons and Trooping Crumble Cap swarmed over the roots of a tree beside the gate on Poplar. I also found three kinds of puffball: on Spinney there was a group of *Bovista plumbea*, a small, sessile species with smooth, white caps; on Peticote, beside the green road hedge, there was a lot of *Vascellum pratense* which has a short stalk and a granular, yellowish cap-surface; and on the trunks and roots of dead elms near the Spinney I came across clusters of the long-stemmed *Lycoperdon pyriforme*. In Brock's Pit I found Weeping Widow and Glistening Ink Cap, both growing from the same rotten and half-buried log, and on the stump of a dead elm, *Rhodotus palmatus*, another species which has only become fairly common since the onset of Dutch Elm disease. It has a rather wrinkled, pinkish orange cap, pale salmony gills and droplets of bright orange, blood-like liquid oozing out from the stems.

Female Dark Bush-cricket.

This was also the time of year when various types of gall became prominent. These are mostly produced by gall wasps (though also by other insects such as sawflies, gall midges and Psyllid bugs), each species having its own very distinctive pattern of gall. The insects inject their eggs into plant tissue and, by some process not yet entirely understood,

Some of the plants still prominent on the meadows in late September. From left to right, Hardheads, Agrimony, False Fox Sedge, Devil's Bit Scabious, Bristly Ox-tongue, Water Figwort and Great Bindweed, with Silver Y Moth.

the plant is prompted to produce an abnormal formation which serves both as food and shelter for the developing larvae. Probably the best-known galls are the Robin's Pincushions which appear in late summer on the leaves of wild roses, starting off green and turning crimson as the autumn advances, but equally common on roses are the much smaller Pea Galls, which may be either smooth or spiked like miniature mines. Both of these were plentiful in the hedgerows, as were the tiny Spangle and Silk Button Galls on the undersides of the oak leaves. I also found hard, round Marble Galls on many of the oak trees and Artichoke Galls on their buds, although there were no signs either of Oak Apple or Knopper Galls, the latter a recently naturalised species which transforms acorns into the semblance of Walnut kernels, and which had been very prevalent the previous year.

During the last week of the month there were some lovely days of typical September weather, starting with pearly-grey misty mornings when the meadows were carpeted with dewy cobwebs and every twig and leaf was hung with sparkling drops of moisture, and developing into warm, balmy afternoons full of the drowsy hum of bees, and evenings when the sunset glow took long to fade and crickets chirped far into the night.

Opposite. A male Common Darter dragonfly perches on a leaf of Branched Bur-reed, which grows in the pond on Rush Meadow.

OCTOBER

Overleaf. A windy day in October: East Meadow, looking eastwards from the gate. On the right is the brook, hidden from view by its fringe of trees and bushes.

*Shaggy Parasol Mushrooms growing under a
Hawthorn bush in the thickets.*

The chief features of October on the meadows were the hordes of mushrooms and toadstools that sprang up in every corner and the wealth of fruit that ripened in the hedges. These hedgerow fruits provided much of the colour, for the leaves were late in turning, and by the end of the month, although some trees, such as the large Willows, were almost bare, the majority were still green, even if splashed here and there with touches of yellow and russet. It was, on the whole, a dry month, with several pleasant Indian summer days and some windy ones, but insufficient rain to induce more than a trickle of water in the upper reaches of the brook.

Fungus growth reached its peak during the first two weeks, which saw a combination of warm sunshine, moist soil and dewy nights. Toadstools came up everywhere, in the woods and thickets, on the banks of the bridleways and all over the meadows. From every visit I would bring back a plastic bag full of specimens for identification, and I spent long hours at my desk sorting them out and trying, frequently without success, to name them.

Field Mushrooms had almost ceased to appear on the meadows by the beginning of the month but Horse Mushrooms were plentiful, notably on Spinney under the oaks, where I would often find rings or groups of up to thirty. Provided they were picked before they became riddled with fungus-gnat maggots, they made excellent eating. The small, delicate fungi scattered all over the meadows were often difficult to identify, but included Liberty Caps, easily recognised by their brown gills and the nipple at the apex of the cap, the attractive, violet coloured form of *Inocybe geophylla*, and *Coprinus niveus*, a species of ink cap which has a mealy white cap-surface and grows on horse dung. Two other species of ink cap that I found growing on Peticote were the Common Ink Cap and the much less common *Coprinus silvaticus*. Most unusual of all, also growing on Peticote in the shade of a large, spreading oak, was *Boletus porosporus*, one of a group of fungi with crowded, vertical tubes under the cap, instead of gills. The notoriously destructive Honey Fungus was abundant in all the wooded parts of the area; it is an irritating species, for it can assume many different forms, and I have often wasted time trying to identify what I took at first to be an unfamiliar species. Also frequent in the woods and bridleways was the rather sinister-looking Verdigris Agaric with its slimy bluish-green cap and cottony stem. It is poisonous, but I cannot imagine anyone being tempted to eat it. In Brock's Pit the many species included Parasol and Shaggy Parasol Mushrooms, Clouded Agaric, Poison Pie and the evil-smelling Stinkhorn; and under the Horse Chestnut trees at the top of the wood there was a fairly widespread colony of the uncommon mushroom *Agaricus vaporarius*. Near by, at the

This fungus, Boletus porosporus, *is an uncommon species. It was growing beneath the spreading branches of an oak tree on Peticote.*

edge of a ploughed field, I found several clusters of bright orange Eyelash Fungus (the contiguity of this and the last-mentioned species in my drawing on page 124 represents a degree of artist's licence).

The greatest glory of the meadows in October was provided by the tall hedgerows all along the green road which carried a mouth-watering abundance of fruit and made a tapestry of rich colour with shades of crimson, scarlet and purple predominating. There were black sloes, with violet-blue bloom, juicy blackberries, broad corymbs of purple elderberries and clusters of jet-black Buckthorn fruits. Hawthorn bushes carried a multitude of crimson haws, and the wild roses were loaded with hips whose hot orange and vermilion tints were matched by those of the Black Bryony berries that hung in ropes from their parent vines. The most vivid and lustrous scarlet was provided by the few Guelder Rose bushes, and touches of shocking pink by the Spindle Tree fruits that would later split open to reveal orange seeds in one of nature's less harmonious conjunctions of colour. Some of the Crab Apple trees carried good crops of little, sour, green or yellow apples, though others were barren, and all the Hazels bore a rich harvest of nuts. Clouds of silvery-grey Old Man's Beard rioted among all this opulence, and creatures of all kinds were already gathering for the great autumnal feast that would give many of them the necessary reserves of fat and energy to carry them through the lean and bitter days ahead.

First among these marauders were the Grey Squirrels which were always to be seen scrambling about the Hazel bushes in search of nuts, or on the meadows collecting fallen acorns. One day, concealed by a screen of leaves in the green road beside Rush Meadow, I spent some time watching one through binoculars as it hopped about the grass, its graceful, flowing movements interrupted by brief periods of absolute stillness as it looked and listened and sniffed the air for any hint of danger. When it found an acorn, it would sit up on its haunches and holding the morsel in its forepaws, nibble at it, perhaps to ensure that the kernel was sound and not withered (my sketch was done as it sat on a fallen branch of oak); then, popping the acorn right into its mouth, it

Opposite. Shaggy Ink-caps, also called Lawyers' Wigs, grow among long grass in the glades on Poplar Meadow.

The shiny, black fruits of Purging Buckthorn which, as
its name implies, was formerly used as a purgative. It
grows in bush form in the green road hedge and as a
small tree in Brock's Pit.

Grey Squirrel.

would bound off towards the base of the hedge, and having found a suitable spot, dig a hole, bury the acorn, cover it and then pat the earth flat. Each acorn was buried in a different spot and I wondered whether winter exhumation was a matter of chance. No doubt many remained buried, only to reappear next year in the form of seedling oaks.

The flowers of Ivy attracted a great many insects including Blue and Green Bottle flies, hover flies, Wasps and Hornets, Honey Bees, Commas and Red Admirals, though there were few of the last in comparison with most years. The Ivy's stratagem of flowering so late in the year, when there is hardly any competition from other flowers, ensures it the most efficient insect pollination service; particularly on the very warm days in the middle of the month, the hum of insects around its flowers, as I walked along the green road, was loud and constant.

It was only towards the end of the month that birds began to make serious inroads on the fruit, with the first flocks of Redwings arriving on the 26th and quickly spreading over the meadows. About the same time House Martins, which, together with Swallows, had vanished from the scene several weeks previously, reappeared in large numbers – travellers, I assumed, from further north. For two or three days they would weave and loop in splendid, exuberant flight over Peticote; then they were off on their long journey to warmer climes.

*Great hordes of Redwings arrive, together with
Fieldfares, in the autumn. This one searches for food —
which includes berries, worms, insects and molluscs —
among a drift of fallen leaves.*

On 4th October I saw a Kestrel over the meadows for the first time. I had been surprised at the absence of this, our only really common and widespread raptor, up to that time, although I would often see one, either perched or hovering beside the lane, as I drove down to the meadows. A week later, near the Spinney, I heard the loud 'tchick, tchick' call of a Great Spotted Woodpecker; shortly afterwards, standing at the base of a dead elm tree, I watched through binoculars and made some sketches of a

Great Spotted
Woodpecker.

*Opposite. The colourful fruits and autumn leaves of the
Spindle tree.*

splendid scarlet-naped male bird as it foraged among the upper branches of the tree, tapping with its powerful beak and occasionally calling. The following week, I was walking beside the hedge on Rush Meadow when a Weasel suddenly popped out of the tussocky grass in front of me, ran a few yards down the hedge, then vanished down a hole in the hedge bottom.

I continued to hear, and sometimes saw, Dark Bush-crickets until the middle of the month, when I also glimpsed my last Southern Hawker dragonfly. On 10th October, I brought home with some fungi a small spider with a shiny black abdomen, orange legs and a bilobed head, which I identified as *Hypomma bituberculatum*. A few days later I noticed a lot of Nettle Groundbugs, both adults and larvae, crowded on the upper leaves of Stinging Nettles on Poplar Meadow; and right at the end of the month by East Meadow, I came across a specimen of the very large green and bronze Hawthorn Shieldbug.

The mushroom Agaricus vaporarius *with fallen Horse Chestnut fruits and a colony of Eyelash Fungus. A rather uncommon species, I found it growing at the southern edge of Brock's Pit.*

Hips of the three species of wild rose to be found on the meadows; left to right Dog Rose, Downy Rose and Field Rose.

NOVEMBER

A pair of Snipe flushed from
the brook on Poplar
Meadow.

During the early days of November the trees and hedgerows around Lapwing Meadows kindled and then blazed with colour. The 10th was a glorious day, warm with only a light breeze and, in the afternoon, a wonderful golden light that enhanced the tints so that the oak trees shone like burnished copper and all the various shades of yellow and amber and red in the woods and hedgerows were lit by points of flame where the low beams of sunlight touched them. There was a mackerel sky, the long, fleecy rows of altocumulus clouds stretching and interlacing across a high dome of milky blue; and as the sun sank towards the west their extremities were drawn out and tossed upwards into graceful mares' tails, and they became tinged with marshmallow-pink.

Fallen Crab Apples and Hawthorn Shieldbug.

I started my walk on Poplar Meadow in the late afternoon, and as I got out of the car my ears were assailed by a cacophony of squawks, wheezes, twitterings and whistles from a great flock of Starlings perched in the tops of the Black Poplar and the trees around it. While I was clambering over the gate into the meadow, the sound was cut off as

Benjamin Perkins 1984

abruptly as if by the baton of a conductor, and a second later the whole flock took wing simultaneously and flew off in the direction of Brock's Pit. I walked beside the hedge, my face caressed by floating strands of invisible gossamer, and in the quiet that followed the Starlings' departure I could hear a Robin singing its sweet, autumnal song from the top of an Ash tree, and further away the resonant song of a Wren. Parties of Black-headed Gulls were drifting overhead, bound for some distant roost, and from all over the meadows there came the chuckling calls of Fieldfares and the thinner notes of Redwings as they foraged among the thickets and hedgerows. To these immigrants from the far north, the meadows, with their rich bounty of fruit, must have seemed like a promised land. Their hordes had started to arrive at the beginning of November, and throughout the month they pillaged and gorged themselves without cease, till there was hardly a hip or a haw or a sloe to be seen. At this date, however, the harvest of fruit seemed hardly to be touched, and it did not seem possible that all of it could be consumed in so short a time.

I walked to the end of Rush Meadow, noting a considerable increase in the number of Pheasants, now that all the crops had been harvested. The undergrowth was starting to die back, too, making them more conspicuous, and young birds were beginning to spread out from the release pens in the woods.

As I turned to come back, the sun was setting with a flourish in the west, the bars of clouds across the empyrean flushed now with a deeper shade of rose, while nearer the horizon the soft-edged cumulus glowed with madder and carmine against a background of brilliant gold. A large flock of Rooks flew slowly overhead, some gliding, some tumbling in play, all of them cawing loudly; Wood Pigeons, too, passed by as they made for their roosts in Brock's Pit and neighbouring woods, their bulging crops prominently silhouetted. Beside the Spinney 'bats were fluttering up and down and there were swarms of dancing gnats that glinted like fireflies in the light of the setting sun. The air smelt of

Previous pages. Spinney Meadow in late November, looking east; on the left oak trees lining the green road, on the right the Spinney, with old Crack Willows in the foreground.

woodsmoke and vegetable decay and new-turned earth (the field below the Lodge was being ploughed) and occasional yellow leaves, dislodged by the breeze, came drifting or spiralling down from the wayside trees. There was the 'chink, chink' of Blackbirds loudly announcing their intention to retire for the night, and the sound of Pheasants 'cocking-up' resounded from every side and was echoed from distant woods. I walked back slowly and by the time I reached the car it was almost dark, though there was still a lurid, violet glow and the odd slash of crimson in the western sky. The last sounds that I heard before starting the engine were the calls and wingbeats of Lapwing as they passed, ghost-like and invisible, overhead.

For the rest of the month the weather remained remarkably mild, although there were a few morning frosts in the last week, and there was sufficient rain to fill the brook and all its tributary ditches. There were several days of high winds which quickly stripped the trees of their finery, so that by the end of the month only the oaks, a few Alders and some of the hedgerow shrubs and woodland under coppice still retained their leaves. The hedgerow fruits were much depleted, though the supply was not yet exhausted, and the Fieldfares and other birds had to work harder to fill their crops.

On 2nd November I had seen the last butterfly of the season – a Small Tortoiseshell – and on the 30th, walking through the thicket glades, I put up the first Woodcock.

Fieldfares arriving.

DECEMBER

Opposite. Black Bryony – the lustrous scarlet fruits glow like jewels in the hedgerows
well into November.

The relatively mild weather continued until almost the end of December. The last leaves fell from the trees, leaving even the oak trees bare, and by the middle of the month the bushes were stripped of nearly all their fruit, and most of the Fieldfares and Red-wings had moved on to other feeding grounds. A few scarlet hips remained on the roses and although the Guelder Rose and Black Bryony berries were largely untouched, all the myriad haws and sloes and elderberries had vanished, and when I chanced upon a hazelnut or an acorn lying in the grass it would almost invariably turn out to be an empty shell. The Brambles, which retained most of their leaves throughout the winter, were still green, and touches of vivid colour were provided, here and there, by the empty pink fruit-husks of the Spindle. Early in the month a few plants were still producing occasional flowers: Red Campion, Hogweed and White Dead-nettle in the hedges, Yarrow and Dandelion on the meadows, and a new crop of Shaggy Parasol Mushrooms came up under the thorn trees in the thickets. In the bridleway between Poplar and East Meadow I found a group of the dark-capped, white-gilled fungus *Melanoleuca melaleuca*, and on dead elms, Hawthorns and other trees, all around the meadows and in the woods, I began to notice clusters of Velvet Shank. This fungus, with its shiny orange-brown caps and velvety purplish-black stems, is one of the most prominent winter-fruiting species, and can survive the severest weather.

December is, superficially at least, a dead month so far as the plant world is concerned: leaves fall, annual plants, having distributed their seeds, die, and perennials are cut back to their rootstocks. Yet in sheltered hollows, there were already the first stirrings of new growth – green shoots poking through the leaf mould, poised to expand and grow as soon as the warmer days of spring gave them encouragement. The bare branches and exposed banks provided a good opportunity to find and examine some of the smaller and less conspicuous plant forms such

Common Cup Lichen, cushions of Curly Thatch Moss and fronds of Cypress-leaved Feather Moss on a tree stump.

as mosses, liverworts, lichens and algae, many of which display their distinctive reproductive processes during the winter months. On 4th December I collected a dozen or so species of moss while walking round the meadows and Brock's Pit, a couple of which I have shown in my drawing. The bright green cushions of Curly Thatch Moss and the neat fronds of Cypress-leaved Feather Moss were growing on a rotten tree stump in the Poplar glades, together with the grey-green scales and goblet-shaped fruiting bodies or podetia of Common Cup Lichen. The latter often grew up through the moss, creating the illusion that they were all parts of the same plant. Near by, on the steep banks of the brook, I found several patches of Crescent-cup Liverwort, a species that I had previously only encountered in gardens and greenhouses, where it is quite common. It is easily recognised by the fact that its dark green 'leaves' bear little crescent-shaped pockets, rather like Swallows' nests, which contain tiny, egg-like reproductive bodies known as gemmae. The patches of liverwort were growing only just above the waterline and were submerged on my next visit when the brook was running high after rain. *Riccardia pinguis*, another liverwort growing in similar situations, occurred further upstream, on Rush, and downstream I found the largest and handsomest species, the Great Scented Liverwort.

Pair of Mallard.

Ben Perkins

Also exposed to view now were many birds' nests left over from the spring. I found plenty of Song Thrushes' and Blackbirds' nests, a Goldfinch's mossy cup on the branch of a Crab Apple, and among others, nests of Willow Warbler, Wren and Long-tailed Tit. In the smallest of the thicket glades, slung between tall grass stems, I came upon the deserted nest of a Harvest Mouse.

Conspicuous on the meadows throughout the month were the Snipe, which were to be found all along the brook, in the marsh and particularly on Rush, where I would sometimes put up thirty or more of them. On 21st December there was a flock of about twenty Golden Plover feeding, together with Lapwing, on Rush, and I would frequently flush a Woodcock or two, particularly from the Blackthorn thickets or the Spinney. Woodcock are crepuscular in their habits and if I were on the meadows at dusk one would often fly overhead, putting me in mind of a great brown moth.

On 27th December there was a hoar frost in the morning and the meadows were sparkling white. As I approached the pond from Spinney Meadow a Kingfisher flashed past within a couple of yards of me, following the line of the brook. It flew just above water level under the overhanging branches of Hazel and Sallow and disappeared towards the Spinney like a tiny blue meteor.

As I came back down the green road hedge on Poplar I disturbed a squirrel on the ground which sprang up into one of the oak trees with a small bird in its mouth. The diet of Grey Squirrels is chiefly vegetable, but they will take meat whenever they can get it, and though birds are generally too agile to be caught, fledglings and birds weakened by prolonged hard weather do provide them with occasional opportunities.

*Opposite. December afternoon: a pair of Mallard rises
up from the pond on Rush Meadow, the duck in the
lead quacking loudly.*

Velvet Shank fungus growing from dead wood at the edge of the Spinney in December.

JANUARY

Wren.

Winter arrived at last, and with a vengeance, early in January. It became very much colder, with winds in the north or north-east, and there were hard frosts at night. The first flurries of snow, which left a fine powdering on the ground, came on the 4th, and three days later, when I had a walk over the meadows, there was an inch of snow on the ground and more falling, fine at first but turning to quite large flakes by the time I left. The brook was frozen over except in stretches where the flow was fast or where it was protected by bushes, and all the standing water – pond, marsh and flashes – was covered by a layer of ice, causing problems for the Snipe, most of which were to be found beside the green road hedge wherever there was a patch of wet ground. Here there was protection from the north, and the sun – which had been out most of the morning – had thawed the ice, allowing them to probe the soil with their long beaks. The frost had not yet penetrated far into the ground, and mounds of dark earth erupting out of the virgin snow indicated that Moles were still able to work the topsoil. A Grey Squirrel, despite the cold, was also active: I saw it hopping about in the hedge bottom on Rush, perhaps searching for the acorns that it had buried there in the autumn. Otherwise the life of the meadows was muted; small birds – Chaffinches, Blackbirds, tits, Robins and Starlings – searched for food among the bare branches of the hedgerows or sat with feathers fluffed against the cold. A few Redwings hunted for any haws that might have been overlooked during the days of plenty, and in the Spinney, twenty or thirty Wood Pigeons had come early to roost off the frozen rape fields. Where the Spinney merged with the marsh I put up two Snipe, a Woodcock and a fine melanistic cock Pheasant that had been scratching and probing in the deep layer of soggy leaf-mould where worms, beetles or buried seeds might still be found.

The hard weather lasted for a fortnight, with frosty nights and many days when the temperature barely rose above freezing. More snow fell, though not to a depth of much more than two inches, and winds remained light so that there was little drifting. My walks on the meadows were made interesting by the many tracks of birds and mammals that were traced in the snow: the prints of a Pheasant that ended between

Opposite. The green road, looking east, with Poplar Meadow on the right, after the first snowfall in January.

deep-scored pinion marks where it had suddenly taken wing, of a vole that had disappeared down a tunnel through a bank of snow, of a fox and a rat that converged on a spatter of blood and the scattered feathers of a Redwing, of squirrels, Mallard, Stoat, small birds and rabbits galore. One solitary and adventurous Field Mouse had set off on a perilous journey across the widest part of Peticote Meadow; I followed the tracks anxiously, imagining the silent swoop of a Tawny Owl that would bring them to an abrupt end but they continued, to my relief, until they were lost among a maze of other trails beneath a Hawthorn bush near the brook.

The thaw came on 21st January, with rain most of the day, and the next day the brook was swollen with melt-water and it overflowed its banks in many places. Within three days all the snow was gone; there was a south-westerly wind and an almost spring-like feeling in the air; Wood Pigeons were chasing each other noisily, and mating, among the Ivy-covered trees in the Spinney, several birds, notably Great Tits, were singing, Alder and Hazel catkins were starting to swell and Bluebells had pushed up bright green spears an inch or two above the ground in the thicket glades. The Bramble leaves, which had remained green until the onset of the hard weather, had now turned a uniform purplish bronze.

For the rest of the month the weather was generally mild and often sunny, giving the meadow creatures a chance to find food once more and replenish their reserves. On the 20th I saw a Kestrel flying over the bridleway from East Meadow to Poplar, and as I walked through the marsh a pair of large, heavy-billed gulls flew overhead – almost certainly Herring Gulls. There were swarms of Winter Gnats dancing above the marsh and I noticed that they were of two kinds: the larger ones with yellowish, banded abdomens belonged to the family Trichoceridae, the smaller ones were Chironomids, dark in colour with humped thoraxes, the males with plumed antennae. I also noted, now that all the vegetation had died down, that most of the marsh had a ground-covering of a handsome golden-green moss, its branch tips forming smooth, cylindrical spikes; I later identified this as Pointed Bog Feather Moss.

Opposite. A twig of Pedunculate Oak with hard,
round Marble Galls and Artichoke (or Hop) Galls on
some of the buds.

FEBRUARY

Opposite. Looking to the west across Poplar Meadow on a frosty February morning, with the two old pollard oaks in the foreground.

Willow Tits are resident on the meadows all year round. This one is perched on a dead branch of Burdock.

The mild weather continued through the first week of February, and the earliest Snowdrops appeared at the bottom of Brock's Pit, their flowers striving to escape from the sheathing leaves almost before they were fairly through the soil. More birds were singing now and as I walked through the thicket glades on 5th February a Marsh or Willow Tit which I had seen there on several occasions without being able to decide on its identity, uttered a short burst of song at just the right moment, and proclaimed itself indisputably as a Willow Tit.

There was a lot of noise that day from the surrounding fields as farmers took advantage of the respite in the weather to get out on the land. To the north of Peticote winter beans were being broadcast on the stubble and ploughed in; from one of the large fields to the south-west came the growl of a tractor applying an early nitrogen top-dressing to the winter wheat; and from Brock's Pit there was the whine of chain saws and the crackle and smoke of a bonfire where fallen elm trees were being cut up and cleared away, and tractors coughed and roared as they hauled heavy loads of logs up the steep rides, leaving deep ruts in their wake.

Three days later it started to snow heavily once again and by evening there was an even covering three or four inches deep. This was followed by hard frosts and a fierce wind blew from the east that caused the snow to drift. When next I managed to get down to the meadows the scene had an austere, arctic beauty. The drifting snow blew off the surrounding fields like white smoke, and on the meadows the drifts had been sculpted by the wind into fantastic shapes, with sharp-edged cliffs, sensuously curving banks and flat surfaces rippled like seashore sand. The trees and bushes, rimed with frost and plastered, on the windward side, with driven snow, stood out in intricate filigree patterns against the leaden sky. Apart from a few gulls sailing across the sky on set wings, there were hardly any signs of life – only a few Blackbirds and the odd Robin and Dunnock that quickly started feeding when I emptied out the contents of my bag of peanuts, breadcrumbs and grated cheese. Icicles drooped from some of the trees and from the overhanging banks of the brook which in places had disappeared entirely under bridges of drifted snow. The deep drifts made progress difficult and it was impossible to face into the cutting wind, laden with stinging snow crystals, so I did not linger.

It remained very cold for about two weeks, but there was little further snow and gradually the drifts, once so pristine, became sullied, their sharp edges slowly eroded by wind and sun. In the wood Dog's Mercury and the furled leaves of Cuckoo Pint thrust up through the snow, and in the tops of the Pussy Willow trees the buds split open to reveal crescents of downy catkin that sparkled with a silvery glint against the blue sky.

The thaw came eventually, and by 24th February most of the snow had gone, with only a few dirty, greyish mounds to show where the deepest drifts had been. It was a lovely day, sunny and warm, and the brook ran high with a cheerful babble and occasional crunching and tinkling sounds as chunks and slivers of half-thawed ice broke free from the banks and went careering downstream.

The Snipe were once more distributed all about the meadows and on Rush I put up some fifteen of them as well as two Green Sandpipers. Fieldfares were feeding out on the meadows, a Lesser Spotted Woodpecker was drumming in the Spinney and many small birds, including a Skylark, were singing. On Peticote, among the crowds of Starlings and

Green Sandpiper.

Lapwing, were five Black-headed Gulls, two of which already had the dark brown hoods of their breeding plumage, and one Common Gull. All over the meadows I found the carcases or scattered feathers of Wood Pigeons that had no doubt succumbed to a shortage of food caused by the hard weather, and in the bridleway by Spinney I found a dead Carrion Crow that had presumably been shot.

Clumps of Snowdrops appear here and there at the bottom of Brock's Pit in February.

Five Black-headed Gulls, two of them already in summer plumage, and one Common Gull.

Near by, from the corner of Rush, I could hear a continuous, low buzzing sound, and when I went through to investigate I was surprised to find numerous Honey Bees all over the ground, their antennae waving up and down and their proboscises probing the damp soil. None were carrying pollen and I could not remember ever seeing them about so early in the year. The nearest hives, so far as I was aware, were just over a mile away. A few days later I saw others, in my garden, on the flowers of Winter Aconites.

I walked across to the brook and waded up it a little way, under the overhanging Hazels, looking for liverworts, and came across a tuft of Male Fern on the bank, the fronds, of course, being left over from the previous summer. Later, as I walked up the bridleway beside Brock's Pit, I happened to notice another tuft of fern at the bottom of the deep ditch that runs between the bridleway and the wood. I was fairly certain that this, too, was Male Fern, but something impelled me to investigate further despite having to climb down the steep sides of the ditch through a mass of very thorny Bramble. I was glad I did so for it turned out to be Hard Prickly Shieldfern, a species which, though common in the country at large, is rare in this county, with only some sixteen records in the *Flora of Essex*.

Having extracted myself from the ditch with some difficulty, I went on to inspect the badger setts which I found in active use with plenty of tracks and a lot of wheat-straw bedding raked back from the mouth of one of them. The straw had obviously been purloined from the pheasant feed beside the ride about twenty yards away. A family of young Badgers was certainly reared in Brock's Pit during the spring, for later in the summer a young male was found dead on the roadside at the top of the wood, having presumably been hit by a passing car.

MARCH

Hen Harrier.

Poplar Meadow, looking east in March. The scene is still a wintry one, and only a closer scrutiny would reveal the first signs of spring.

On a very windy day in early March, several years before starting the present survey, I had my most exciting encounter on the meadows. I had parked the car on the road above Brock's Pit, and was walking down the bridleway when suddenly, breasting the wind in agile and graceful flight, a female Hen Harrier appeared over the wheat field to my left. Alternating a few powerful wing-beats with long glides, she flew down to the far end of Peticote and then returned, quartering low over the meadows. For a time she disappeared and then I saw her again over Poplar where she flew up and settled in the top of an Ash tree. I had excellent views of her, noting her dark brown colouring and streaked underparts, the long, barred tail and the white crescent on her rump. As I approached, she spread her wings and lifted to a gust of wind and then went slanting away across the green road, quickly vanishing over the fields to the north.

This year March provided no special thrills. It was, despite a few fine days early in the month, when the Hazel bushes in Brock's Pit were alive with Honey Bees collecting pollen from the ripe catkins, a preponderantly wintry month, with dull, damp and windy days interspersed with a disagreeable assortment of rain, hail, sleet and snow showers. One more bird species for the record was provided by a pair of Pied Wagtails that were feeding, on 4th March, under the big oaks on Poplar, where the horses are normally fed. A pair of Lapwing were already displaying and uttering their distinctive spring calls on the 14th, when I also noted a pair of Collared Turtle Doves flying into a tree in the East Meadow hedge. I often saw drake Mallard in each other's company, indicating that the ducks were sitting. A Blackbird was hard at work nest-building on 21st March and I noticed Wrens all over the meadows, suggesting that the successive spells of severe weather had not been sufficiently protracted to cull their numbers appreciably, as sometimes happens in hard winters. Treecreepers were also in evidence, and it was while watching one, on the 25th, that I noticed, in the same Alder tree, the first Redpolls of the year. They were feeding on Alder seeds all along the brook on Poplar and Peticote, but it was hard to tell how many as they kept flying on ahead of me – perhaps a dozen or fourteen altogether. As I walked through the thicket glades I heard the 'sip, sip' calls of Siskins which were also present in good numbers; they and the Redpolls seemed to be in separate flocks but mingled together as they fed.

Coltsfoot flowered by the brook in the thicket glades and towards the end of the month I saw the first Sweet Violets and Red Dead-nettle in flower on East Meadow. There was also a flush of rusty crimson here and there in the hedgerows where the few remaining small elm trees were in flower, and other promises of the burgeoning soon to come were provided by the swelling red buds on the wild roses and tufts of dull green young leaves on the Elders.

It was not until the last day of the month that the weather gave any real indication of winter being over. The sun shone and the wind veered round from the north to the south-west. Basking in the unaccustomed warmth, I could almost imagine the meadow plants growing before my eyes. Beside the hedge on East Meadow the Primroses decided that at last the time was ripe to open their pale yellow flowers and greet the spring; and, as if encouraged by their example, the first butterfly, a Small Tortoiseshell, emerged from its long hibernation in some cobwebby crevice, and came fluttering down the meadow in feckless, carefree flight, rising exultantly above the treetops as it passed into Poplar Meadow.

In March the pale, lemon-yellow flowers and the
crinkled, green leaves of the Primrose brighten the
hedgerows, brookside and the banks of the bridleways.

Opposite. Coltsfoot just starting to flower about the
middle of March, and an early Honey Bee.

SYSTEMATIC LIST OF SPECIES

The species listed below, grouped for convenience into eight main categories, are those which have been mentioned in the text as having been identified, either definitely or in a few cases doubtfully, on or over Lapwing Meadows and the adjoining woods. Species followed by a page reference are illustrated in the book.

I have tried to give the most up-to-date scientific names, but changes in nomenclature have come thick and fast in recent years, and no doubt some of these changes will have been missed.

1. MAMMALS
Badger *Meles meles: 18*
Bat, Noctule *Nyctalus noctula*
Bat, Pipistrelle *Pipistrellus pipistrellus: 46*
Deer, Roe *Capreolus capreolus*
Fox *Vulpes vulpes: 40*
Hare *Lepus capensis*
Hedgehog *Erinaceus europaeus: 65*
Mole *Talpa europaea*

Mouse, Field *Apodemus sylvaticus*
Mouse, Harvest *Micromys minutus*
Rabbit *Oryctolagus cuniculus: 7*
Rat, Brown *Rattus norvegicus*
Stoat *Mustela erminea: 93*
Squirrel, Grey *Neosciurus carolinensis: 119*
Vole, Short-tailed *Microtus agrestis*
Weasel *Mustela nivalis*

2. BIRDS
Blackbird *Turdus merula*
Blackcap *Sylvia atricapilla*
Bullfinch *Pyrrhula pyrrhula*
Bunting, Reed *Emberiza schoeniclus: 33*
Chaffinch *Fringilla coelebs*
Chiffchaff *Phylloscopus collybita*
Crow, Carrion *Corvus corone*
Cuckoo *Cuculus canorus*
Dove, Collared Turtle *Streptopelia decaocto*
Dove, Stock *Columba oenas*
Dove, Turtle *Streptopelia turtur*
Dunnock *Prunella modularis*
Fieldfare *Turdus pilaris: 131*
Flycatcher, Spotted *Muscicapa striata*
Goldcrest *Regulus regulus*
Goldfinch *Carduelis carduelis*
Greenfinch *Carduelis chloris*
Gull, Black-headed *Larus ridibundus: 150*
Gull, Common *Larus canus: 150*
Gull, Herring *Larus argentatus*
Harrier, Hen *Circus cyaneus: 151*
Heron, Grey *Ardea cinerea: 98-9*
Jay *Garrulus glandarius*
Kestrel *Falco tinnunculus*
Kingfisher *Alcedo atthis: 25*
Lapwing *Vanellus vanellus: 49*
Linnet *Carduelis cannabina*
Magpie *Pica pica*
Mallard *Anas platyrhynchos: 135-6*
Martin, House *Delichon urbica*
Moorhen *Gallinula chloropus*
Owl, Tawny *Strix aluco: 145*
Partridge, Red-legged *Alectoris rufa*
Pheasant *Phasianus colchicus*
Plover, Golden *Pluvialis apricaria*

Rail, Water *Rallus aquaticus*
Redpoll *Carduelis flammea: 10*
Redwing *Turdus iliacus: 120-1*
Robin *Erithacus rubecula*
Rook *Corvus frugilegus*
Sandpiper, Green *Tringa ochropus: 148*
Siskin *Carduelis spinus: 10*
Skylark *Alauda arvensis*
Snipe *Gallinago gallinago: 126*
Sparrow, House *Passer domesticus*
Sparrow, Tree *Passer montanus*
Starling *Sturnus vulgaris*
Swallow *Hirundo rustica*
Swift *Apus apus*
Tern, Common *Sterna hirundo*
Thrush, Mistle *Turdus viscivorus*
Thrush, Song *Turdus philomelos*
Tit, Blue *Parus caeruleus*
Tit, Coal *Parus ater*
Tit, Great *Parus major*
Tit, Long-tailed *Aegithalos caudatus: 23*
Tit, Marsh *Parus palustris*
Tit, Willow *Parus montanus: 146*
Treecreeper *Certhia familiaris: Half title*
Wagtail, Pied *Motacilla alba*
Warbler, Garden *Sylvia borin*
Warbler, Willow *Phylloscopus trochilus*
Whitethroat *Sylvia communis*
Woodcock *Scolopax rusticola*
Woodpecker, Great Spotted *Dendrocopos major: 122*
Woodpecker, Green *Picus viridis*
Woodpecker, Lesser Spotted *Dendrocopos minor*
Wood Pigeon *Columba palumbus: 19*
Wren *Troglodytes troglodytes: 139*
Yellowhammer *Emberiza citrinella*

3. FISH, AMPHIBIANS AND REPTILES
Miller's Thumb *Cottus gobio*
Newt, Smooth *Triturus vulgaris*

Snake, Grass *Natrix natrix: 92*
Stickleback, Three-spined *Gasterosteus aculeatus: 31*

4 BUTTERFLIES AND MOTHS
  (a) Butterflies
Admiral, Red *Vanessa atalanta: 100*
Blue, Common *Polyommatus icarus: 88*
Blue, Holly *Celastrina argiolus: 88*
Brimstone *Gonepteryx rhamni: 102*
Brown, Meadow *Maniola jurtina: 68*
Brown, Wall *Pararge megera*
Comma *Polygonia c-album*
Copper, Small *Lycaena phlaes: 75*
Gatekeeper *Pyronia tithonus*
Hairstreak, Purple *Quercusia quercus*

Heath, Small *Coenonympha pamphilus*
Orange-tip *Anthocharis cardamines: 54*
Painted Lady *Vanessa cardui: 97*
Peacock *Inachis io: 34*
Skipper, Large *Ochlodes venata*
Skipper, Small *Thymelicus sylvestris: 15*
Tortoiseshell, Small *Aglais urticae: 88*
White, Green-veined *Pieris napi: 30*
White, Large *Pieris brassicae: 94*
White, Small *Pieris rapae*

  (b) Moths
Angle Shades *Phlogophora meticulosa*
Buff-tip *Phalera bucephala: 105*
Carpet, Silver Ground *Xanthorhoe montanata*
Ermine, Muslin *Cycnia mendica*
Footman, Common *Eilema lurideola*
Golden Y, Plain *Plusia jota*
Mother-of-Pearl *Pleuroptya ruralis*
Peach Blossom *Thyatira batis*

Plume Moths *Family Pterophoridae*
Prominent, Coxcomb *Lophopteryx capucina*
Shark, Mullein *Cucullia verbasci*
Silver Y *Plusia gamma: 107*
Thorn, Canary-shouldered *Deuteronomos alniuria*
Underwing, Copper *Amphipyra pyramidaea*
Wainscot, Common *Leucania pallens*

5. INSECTS OTHER THAN BUTTERFLIES AND MOTHS
Alderfly *Sialis sp.*
Bee, Common Carder *Bombus agrorum*
Bee, Honey *Apis mellifera: 155*
Bee, Red-shanked Carder *Bombus derhamellus*
Bee, Vestal Cuckoo *Psithyrus vestalis*
Bee Fly *Bombylius major*
Beetle *Chrysolina sp.*
Beetle, Cardinal *Pyrochroa serraticornis*
Beetle, Lesser Stag *Dorcus parallelopipedus*
Beetle, Soldier *Rhagonycha fulva*
Beetle, Wasp *Clytus arietis*
Beetle, Whirligig *Family Gyrinidae*
Blue Bottle *Calliphora vomitoria*
Bug *Deraeocoris ruber*
Bumble Bee, *see* Humble Bee
Bush-cricket, Dark *Pholidoptera griseoaptera: 106*
Bush-cricket, Oak *Meconema thalassinum*
Bush-cricket, Speckled *Leptophyes punctatissima: 84*
Cleg *Haematopota pluvialis*
Crane Fly *Family Tipulidae*
Cricket, *see* Bush-cricket
Damselfly, Azure *Coenagrion puella: 15*
Damselfly, Banded Demoiselle *Calopteryx splendens*
Damselfly, Blue-tailed *Ischnura elegans*

Dragonfly, Broad-bodied Chaser *Libellula depressa: 53*
Dragonfly, Brown Hawker *Aeshna grandis*
Dragonfly, Common Darter *Sympetrum striolatum: 108*
Dragonfly, Southern Hawker *Aeshna cyanea: 64*
Drone Fly *Volucella bombylans*
Drone Fly *Volucella pellucens*
Earwig *Family Forficulidae*
Fly *Empis tessellata*
Froghopper *Cercopis vulnerata*
Fungus Gnat *Family Mycetophilidae*
Gall Wasp, Artichoke *Andricus fecundator: 143*
Gall Wasp, Oak Marble *Andricus kollari: 143*
Gall Wasp, Pea *Diplolepis nervosa: 6*
Gall Wasp, Robin's Pincushion *Diplolepis rosae: 6*
Gall Wasp, Silk Button *Neuroterus numismatis*
Gall Wasp, Spangle *Neuroterus quercusbaccarum*
Gnat *Family Trichoceridae*
Green Bottle *Orthellia caesarion*
Groundbug, Nettle *Heterogaster urticae*
Hornet *Vespa crabro*
Humble Bee, Buff-tailed *Bombus terrestris*
Humble Bee, Large Red-tailed *Bombus lapidarius*

Humble Bee, Small Earth *Bombus lucorum*
Humble Bee, Small Garden *Bombus hortorum: 73*
Lacewing, Green *Chrysopa sp.*
Ladybird Beetle, 7-spot *Coccinella 7-punctata: 88*
Ladybird Beetle, 22-spot *Psyllobora 22-punctata*
Ladybird Beetle, 2-spot *Adalia bipunctata*
Leafhopper *Family Cicadellidae*
Mayfly, Pond Olive *Cloeon dipterum*
Midge *Family Chironomidae*
Midge, Phantom *Chaoborus crystallinus*
Pond Skater *Gerris lacustris*

6. INVERTEBRATES OTHER THAN INSECTS
Crustacean *Cyclops sp.*
Harvestman *Leiobunum rotundum*
Shrimp, Freshwater *Gammarus sp.*
Snail *Cepaea nemoralis: 90*
Snail *Monacha cantiana: 90*
Snail *Oxyloma pfeifferi: 61*
Snail *Trichia hispida*
Snail, Garden *Helix aspersa: 28*

7. FLOWERING PLANTS
Agrimony, Common *Agrimonia eupatoria: 107*
Agrimony, Hemp *Eupatorium cannabinum: 75*
Alder *Alnus glutinosa*
Angelica, Wild *Angelica sylvestris*
Apple, Crab *Malus sylvestris: 127*
Ash *Fraxinus excelsior*
Bartsia, Red *Odontites verna: 88*
Basil, Wild *Clinopodium vulgare*
Bedstraw, Lady's *Galium verum*
Bedstraw, Marsh *Galium palustre*
Bellflower, Nettle-leaved *Campanula trachelium: 86*
Bent, Common *Agrostis capillaris*
Bent, Creeping *Agrostis stolonifera*
Bindweed, Great *Calystegia silvatica: 107*
Bindweed, Lesser *Convolvulus arvensis: 68*
Bird's-foot Trefoil, Common *Lotus corniculatus: 88*
Bird's-foot Trefoil, Marsh *Lotus uliginosus: 15*
Blackthorn *Prunus spinosa*
Bluebell *Endymion non-scriptus*
Bramble *Rubus fruticosus: 100*
Brome Grass, Soft *Bromus hordeaceus*
Brome Grass, Woodland *Bromus ramosus*
Brooklime *Veronica beccabunga: 53*
Bryony, Black *Tamus communis: 132*
Bryony, White *Bryonia dioica*
Buckthorn, Purging *Rhamnus catharticus: 118*
Bugle *Ajuga reptans: 44*
Burdock, Common *Arctium pubens: 146*
Bur-reed, Branched *Sparganium erectum: 108*
Buttercup, Creeping *Ranunculus repens*

Scorpion Fly *Panorpa sp.*
Shieldbug *Eysarcoris fabricii: 30*
Shieldbug, Hawthorn *Acanthosoma haemorrhoidale: 127*
Shieldbug, Pied *Sehirus bicolor*
Soldier Fly *Chloromyia formosa*
Thrips *Order Thysanoptera*
Wasp, Common *Vespula vulgaris*
Wasp, Ruby-tailed *Chrysis ignita*
Water Beetle *Acilius sulcatus*
Water Boatman *Notonecta glauca*

Spider *Enoplognatha ovata*
Spider *Hypomma bituberculatum*
Spider *Nuctenea cornuta*
Spider *Pisaura mirabilis*
Spider, Crab *Misumena vatia*
Spider, Jumping *Family Salticidae*
Spider, Wolf *Family Lycosidae*

Buttercup, Meadow *Ranunculus acris: 41*
Campion, Red *Silene dioica*
Campion, White *Silene pratense*
Canary Grass, Reed *Phalaris arundinacea*
Cat's-ear, Common *Hypochoeris radicata*
Celandine, Lesser *Ranunculus ficaria*
Centaury, Common *Centaurium erythraea*
Chamomile, Rayless *Chamomilla suaveolens*
Chervil *Chaerophyllum temulentum*
Chestnut, Horse *Aesculus hippocastanum: 124*
Chickweed, Common Mouse-ear *Cerastium fontanum*
Chickweed, Water *Myosoton aquaticum*
Cinquefoil, Creeping *Potentilla reptans*
Cleavers *Galium aparine*
Clover, Alsike *Trifolium hybridum*
Clover, Red *Trifolium pratense: 54*
Clover, White *Trifolium repens: 54*
Cocksfoot *Dactylis glomerata*
Coltsfoot *Tussilago farfara: 154*
Couch Grass, Common *Elymus repens*
Cowslip *Primula veris: 34*
Cranesbill, Cut-leaved *Geranium dissectum*
Cranesbill, Dove's Foot *Geranium molle*
Creeping Jenny *Lysimachia nummularia: Title page*
Cress, Water *Nasturtium officinale: 53*
Crowfoot, Celery-leaved *Ranunculus sceleratus*
Crowfoot, Pond Water *Ranunculus peltatus*
Cuckoo Flower *Cardamine pratensis: 41*
Cuckoo Pint *Arum maculatum: 39, 90*
Currant, Red *Ribes rubrum*

Daisy *Bellis perennis: 34*
Dandelion *Taraxacum officinale: 43*
Dead-nettle, Red *Lamium purpureum: 28*
Dead-nettle, White *Lamium album*
Dock, Broad-leaved *Rumex obtusifolius*
Dock, Curled *Rumex crispus*
Dock, Red-veined *Rumex sanguineus: 88*
Dogstail, Crested *Cynosurus cristatus*
Dogwood *Cornus sanguinea*
Duckweed, Lesser *Lemna minor*
Elder *Sambucus nigra*
Elm, Smooth-leaved *Ulmus carpinifolia*
Elm, Wych *Ulmus glabra*
Fat-hen *Chenopodium album*
Fescue, Meadow *Festuca pratensis*
Figwort, Common *Scrophularia nodosa*
Figwort, Water *Scrophularia auriculata: 107*
Fleabane, Common *Pulicaria dysenterica: 88*
Forget-me-not, Common *Myosotis arvensis*
Foxtail, Meadow *Alopecurus pratensis*
Gipsywort *Lycopus europaeus*
Goosefoot, Red *Chenopodium rubrum*
Grass, Flote *Glyceria fluitans*
Grass, Sweet Vernal *Anthoxanthum odoratum: 30*
Ground Ivy *Glechoma hederacea: 30, 34*
Groundsel *Senecio vulgaris*
Hardheads *Centaurea nigra: 107*
Hawk's-beard, Beaked *Crepis polymorpha*
Hawk's-beard, Rough *Crepis biennis*
Hawk's-beard, Smooth *Crepis capillaris: 68*
Hawthorn *Crataegus monogyna*
Hazel *Corylus avellana*
Hemlock *Conium maculatum*
Herb Bennet *Geum urbanum*
Herb Robert *Geranium robertianum*
Hogweed *Heracleum sphondylium*
Hop *Humulus lupulus*
Horehound, Black *Ballota nigra: 70*
Hound's Tongue *Cynoglossum officinale: 45*
Iris, Yellow Flag *Iris pseudocorus: 59*
Ivy *Hedera helix*
Kingcup *Caltha palustris 20*
Knapweed, Greater *Centaurea scabiosa: 88*
Knotgrass, Common *Polygonum aviculare*
Larch, European *Larix decidua*
Lady's Smock, *see* Cuckoo Flower
Lettuce, Prickly *Lactuca serriola*
Loosestrife, Purple *Lythrum salicaria: 88*
Lords and Ladies, *see* Cuckoo Pint
Mallow, Common *Malva sylvestris*
Maple, Field *Acer campestre*
Marigold, Marsh, *see* Kingcup
Marshwort, Procumbent *Apium nodiflorum*

Mayweed, Scentless *Matricaria perforata*
Meadow Grass, Annual *Poa annua*
Meadow Grass, Smooth *Poa pratensis*
Meadowsweet *Filipendula ulmaria: 88*
Medick, Black *Medicago lupulina: 54*
Melilot, Yellow *Melilotus altissima*
Mercury, Dog's *Mercurialis perennis*
Mint, Pepper *Mentha x piperita*
Mint, Water *Mentha aquatica: 15*
Mugwort *Artemisia vulgaris*
Mullein, Common *Verbascum thapsus*
Mustard, Garlic *Alliaria petiolata*
Mustard, Hedge *Sisymbrium officinale*
Nettle, Stinging *Urtica dioica*
Nightshade, Woody *Solanum dulcamara*
Nipplewort *Lapsana communis*
Oak, Common, *see* Oak, Pedunculate
Oak, Pedunculate *Quercus robur: 81*
Old Man's Beard, *see* Traveller's Joy
Orchid, Common Spotted *Dactylorhiza fuchsii ssp. fuchsii: 50*
Orchid, Southern Marsh *Dactylorhiza majalis spp. praetermissa: 50*
Ox-tongue, Bristly *Picris echioides: 107*
Parsley, Cow *Anthriscus sylvestris*
Parsley, Hedge *Torilis japonica*
Pimpernel, Scarlet *Anagallis arvensis*
Plantain, Great *Plantago major*
Plantain, Ribwort *Plantago lanceolata*
Plantain, Water *Alisma plantago-aquatica*
Poplar, Black *Populus nigra: 13*
Poplar, Black Italian *Populus 'Serotina'*
Poppy, Field *Papaver rhoeas*
Primrose *Primula vulgaris: 155*
Ragged Robin *Lychnis flos-cuculi: 61*
Ragwort, Common *Senecio jacobaea: 102*
Ragwort, Hoary *Senecio erucifolius: 102*
Redshank *Polygonum persicaria*
Rocket, Dyer's *Reseda luteola*
Rocket, Yellow *Barbarea vulgaris*
Rose, Dog *Rosa canina: 57, 125*
Rose, Downy *Rosa tomentosa: 125*
Rose, Field *Rosa arvensis: 125*
Rose, Guelder *Viburnum opulus*
Rush, Hard *Juncus inflexus*
Rush, Jointed *Juncus articulatus*
Rush, Soft *Juncus effusus*
Rush, Toad *Juncus bufonius*
Ryegrass, Perennial *Lolium perenne*
St John's-wort, Perforate *Hypericum perforatum*
St John's-wort, Square-stalked *Hypericum tetrapterum*
Sallow *Salix caprea*

Scabious, Devil's Bit *Succisa pratensis: 107*
Scabious, Field *Knautia arvensis: 88*
Scirpus, Bristle *Scirpus setaceus*
Sedge, False Fox *Carex otrubae: 107*
Sedge, Glaucous *Carex flacca*
Sedge, Hairy *Carex hirta*
Sedge, Lesser Pond *Carex acutiforma*
Self-heal *Prunella vulgaris: 68*
Shepherd's Purse *Capsella bursa-pastoris*
Snowdrop *Galanthus nivalis: 149*
Sowthistle, Corn *Sonchus arvensis*
Sowthistle, Prickly *Sonchus asper*
Speedwell, Germander *Veronica chamaedrys: 38*
Speedwell, Grey *Veronica polita*
Speedwell, Pink Water *Veronica catenata*
Speedwell, Thyme-leaved *Veronica serpyllifolia*
Speedwell, Water *Veronica anagallis-aquatica*
Spindle *Euonymus europaeus: 123*
Spruce, Norway *Picea abies*
Starwort, Common Water *Callitriche stagnalis*
Stitchwort, Greater *Stellaria holostea*
Stitchwort, Lesser *Stellaria graminea*
Sycamore *Acer pseudoplatanus*
Teasel *Dipsacus fullonum*

Thistle, Field *Cirsium arvense*
Thistle, Marsh *Cirsium palustre*
Thistle, Spear *Cirsium vulgare: 83*
Thistle, Welted *Carduus crispus*
Timothy *Phleum pratense*
Traveller's Joy *Clematis vitalba: 100*
Trefoil, Hop *Trifolium campestre: 54*
Trefoil, Lesser Yellow *Trifolium dubium*
Vetch, Bush *Vicia sepium*
Vetch, Tufted *Vicia cracca: 94*
Vetchling, Yellow Meadow *Lathyrus pratensis: 15*
Violet, Early Dog *Viola reichenbachiana: 32*
Violet, Hairy *Viola hirta: 32*
Violet, Sweet *Viola odorata: 28, 32*
Willow, Crack *Salix fragilis*
Willow, Pussy, *see* Sallow
Willow, White *Salix alba*
Willow-herb, Great Hairy *Epilobium hirsutum*
Willow-herb, Lesser Hairy *Epilobium parviflorum*
Woodrush, Field *Luzula campestris: 34*
Woundwort, Hedge *Stachys sylvatica: 73*
Yarrow *Achillea millefolium: 88*
Yorkshire Fog *Holcus lanatus*

8. NON-FLOWERING PLANTS
(a) Fungi

Agaric, Clouded *Clitocybe nebularis*
Agaric, Verdigris *Stropharia aeruginosa*
Cramp Ball *Daldinia concentrica*
Eyelash Fungus *Scutellinia scutellata: 124*
Fairy Ring Champignon *Marasmius oreades*
Fungus *Agaricus vaporarius: 124*
Fungus *Bolbitius vitellinus*
Fungus *Boletus porosporus: 115*
Fungus *Coprinus silvaticus*
Fungus *Inocybe geophylla var. lilacina*
Fungus *Melanoleuca melaleuca*
Fungus *Panaeolus semiovatus*
Fungus *Pleurotus cornucopiae: dedication page*
Fungus *Rhodotus palmatus*
Honey Fungus *Armillaria mellea*
Ink Cap, Common *Coprinus atramentarius*

Ink Cap, Glistening *Coprinus micaceus*
Ink Cap, Shaggy *Coprinus comatus: 116*
Liberty Cap *Psilocybe semilanceata*
Mushroom, Field *Agaricus campestris: 103*
Mushroom, Horse *Agaricus arvensis*
Mushroom, Parasol *Lepiota procera*
Mushroom, Shaggy Parasol *Lepiota rhacodes: 111*
Poison Pie *Hebeloma crustuliniforme*
Puffball *Bovista plumbea*
Puffball *Lycoperdon pyriforme*
Puffball *Vascellum pratense*
Stinkhorn *Phallus impudicus*
Trooping Crumble Cap *Coprinus disseminatus*
Velvet Shank *Flammulina velutipes: 138*
Weeping Widow *Lacrymaria velutina*

(b) Ferns, Horsetails, Mosses, Liverworts and Lichens

Bracken *Pteridium aquilinum*
Fern, Male *Dryopteris filix-mas*
Horsetail, Marsh *Equisetum palustre*
Lichen, Common Cup *Cladonia fimbriata: 134*
Liverwort *Riccardia pinguis*
Liverwort, Crescent-cup *Lunularia cruciata*
Liverwort, Great Scented *Conocephalum conicum*
Moss, Curly Thatch *Dicranoweissia cirrata: 134*

Moss, Cypress-leaved Feather *Hypnum cupressiforme: 134*
Moss, Fox-tail Feather *Thamnobryum alopecurum*
Moss, Pointed Bog Feather *Acroladium cuspidatum*
Moss, Tamarisk-leaved Feather *Thuidium tamariscinum*
Shieldfern, Hard Prickly *Polystichum aculeatum*

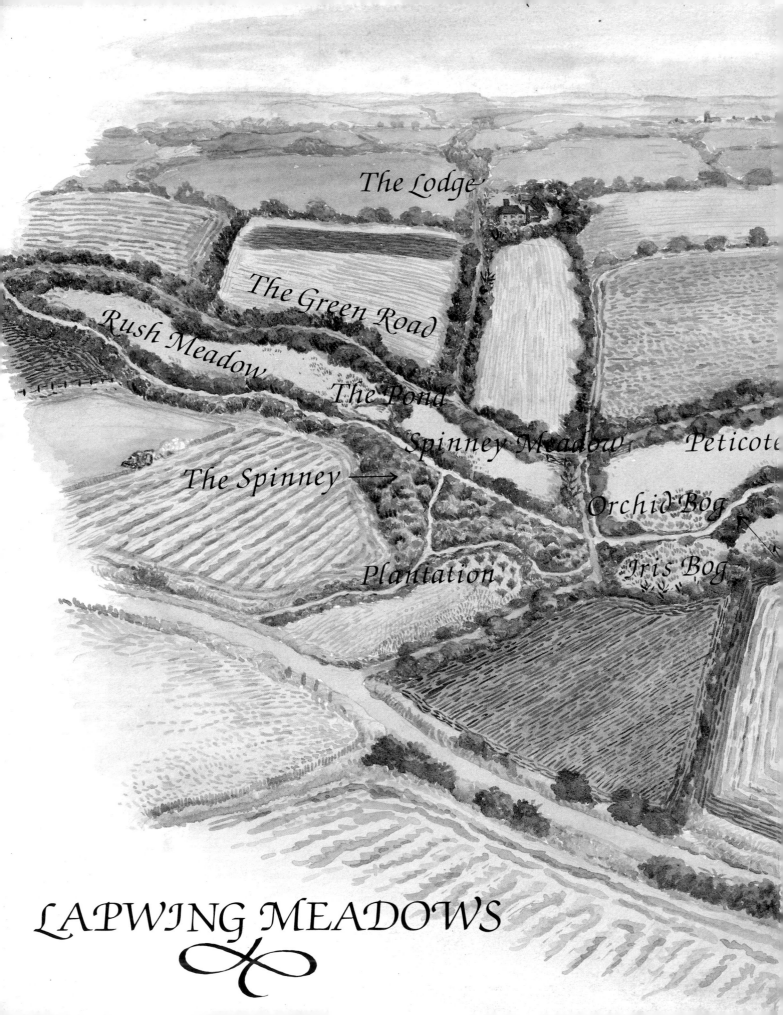

The Lodge

The Green Road

Rush Meadow

The Pond

The Spinney →

Spinney Meadow

Peticote

The Spinney

Orchid Bog

Plantation

Iris Bog

LAPWING MEADOWS